# KYLIE MINOGUE
# BIOGRAPHY

## A Life in Music, Style, and Reinvention

By

Jamie M. Beverly

Copyright © **Jamie M. Beverly**, 2024

All rights reserved.

No part of this publication may be replicated, distributed, or transmitted in any manner, including photocopying, recording, or any electronic or mechanical means, without prior written authorization from the publisher, except for brief quotations included in critical reviews or specific noncommercial uses allowed by copyright law.

Disclaimer: This book contains information that is solely meant to be educational. Despite their best efforts to present accurate and current information, the author and publisher disclaim all expressed and implied representations and warranties regarding the availability, completeness, accuracy, reliability, suitability, or suitability of the content contained herein for any purpose. The publisher and the author disclaim all responsibility for any loss or harm, including without limitation, consequential or indirect loss or damage, or any loss or damage at all resulting from lost profits or data resulting from using this book

# Table of contents

INTRODUCTION

CHAPTER 1: WHO IS KYLIE MINOGUE?

CHAPTER 2: KYLIE'S SCHOOLING DAYS

CHAPTER 3: STEPPING INTO THE SPOTLIGHT: EARLY ACTING CAREER

CHAPTER 4: THE LEAP INTO MUSIC

CHAPTER 5: GLOBAL STARDOM AND POP SUCCESS

CHAPTER 6: EVOLVING AS AN ARTIST

CHAPTER 7: BREAKING THE MOLD: THE 1990s TRANSFORMATION

CHAPTER 8: THE 2000s COMEBACK AND GLOBAL DOMINANCE

CHAPTER 9: BATTLING ADVERSITY: OVERCOMING BREAST CANCER

CHAPTER 10: FASHION AND STYLE ICON

CHAPTER 11: PERSONAL LIFE AND RELATIONSHIPS

CHAPTER 12: PHILANTHROPY AND PUBLIC INFLUENCE

CHAPTER 13: MUSICAL LONGEVITY AND INNOVATION

CHAPTER 14: CULTURAL IMPACT AND GAY ICON STATUS

CHAPTER 15: AWARDS, HONORS, AND MILESTONES

CHAPTER 16: KYLIE MINOGUE: A LIFE BEYOND THE STAGE

CONCLUSION

# INTRODUCTION

The name Kylie Minogue is a byword for persistence, reinvention, and worldwide pop music triumph. One of the most amazing tales in contemporary entertainment is her transformation from a young TV actress to a global music phenomenon. After more than thirty years in the public eye, Kylie's capacity to adjust to shifting fads and preferences has solidified her place as a timeless figure in the music, fashion, and popular culture industries. Kylie's ability to continuously reinvent herself and remain relevant during times when many others have faltered is what makes her stand out. Her development from her early bubblegum pop beginnings to the seductive and elegant performer she became in the 1990s is evidence of both her dedication to invention and her own personal development. Although Kylie's early appearances on the well-liked Australian serial opera Neighbours helped to make her famous, her bold entry into the music industry was what really made her name. Even though her first single, "The Locomotion," was a huge hit, her remarkable career trajectory was just getting started. In addition to creating timeless classics over the course of her career, Kylie has established a reputation for tenacity.

From the financial highs and lows of her albums in the 1990s to her intensely personal fight with breast cancer in 2005, her journey has not been without its challenges. She has overcome every obstacle with a fresh sense of purpose, coming back to the stage and studio with more poise and tenacity than before. Because of this spirit, Kylie has become more than just a pop star; she is now a genuine cultural phenomenon. Kylie's genuineness and adaptability are what make her so appealing. In addition to being a musician, she is also a style icon and a representation of tenacity. Her influence on the fashion industry is undeniable, as her daring decisions have shaped designers and trends for many years. Generations of fans have been won over by Kylie's charm and charisma, and her enduring popularity in a field that is always changing says a lot about her talent and ambition. The entirety of Kylie Minogue's life is covered in this biography, which includes an examination of her early years, ascent to prominence, and difficulties encountered during her career. It delves deeply into her role as a fashion trailblazer, her continuing effect on pop culture around the world, and the challenges of managing a constantly shifting music industry. From her modest upbringing in Melbourne to her rise to global fame, Kylie Minogue's story is one of success, rebirth, and unrelenting love for what she does. Every phase of her work reflects her continuous development as an artist rather than merely a change in sound or style. The sum of Kylie's career, not just one particular instance or accomplishment, defines her legacy. She has inspired innumerable people worldwide with her music, live appearances, and personal struggles. Kylie Minogue is an artist whose impact will continue to change the entertainment world for centuries to come, and this biography attempts to document her incredible life.

# CHAPTER 1: WHO IS KYLIE MINOGUE?

Australia's Kylie Minogue is a singer, songwriter, and actress who rose to international prominence in the late 1980s and is now among the most successful pop musicians of her cohort. She initially gained notoriety as an actor, playing the lead in the well-liked Australian serial show Neighbours, but her singing career brought her to a global audience. Kylie began a lengthy and fruitful career in music in 1987 after releasing her first single, "The Loco-Motion," which became an enormous smash. She is well-known for fusing disco with dance-pop, and she has generated a number of successes, including "Love at First Sight," "Spinning Around," and "Can't Get You Out of My Head." Thanks to her many years of popularity, Kylie has become a pop icon, particularly in Australia and Europe. Minogue's career has sold over 80 million records worldwide and earned her multiple accolades, including a Grammy and Brit Awards. In addition to her singing, she has acted in movies and occasionally still does. Thanks to her impact on pop music, fashion, and society, she has gained international acclaim and is frequently referred to as the "Princess of Pop."

## Growing Up in Melbourne, Australia (Born May 28, 1968)

On May 28, 1968, Kylie Ann Minogue was born in Melbourne, Australia. Melbourne was a developing metropolis at the time, renowned for its thriving arts scene, multicultural populace, and cultural vibrancy. Melbourne, which is in the state of Victoria, provided Kylie with the ideal environment for her early years and the emergence of her first creative ideas. Because the Minogue family lived in the suburbs, Kylie was able to enjoy both the calm, nurturing atmosphere of suburbia life and the urban richness of Melbourne's city life. Early in life, Kylie lived in the quiet yet vibrant suburban communities of Surrey Hills and Camberwell. These were tight-knit neighborhoods where neighbors knew one another and kids were free to roam the streets, full of imagination and curiosity. She was able to gain independence and a sense of self in this supportive setting, which was crucial for her developing creativity. Melbourne saw expansion and change in the late 1960s and early 1970s.

Due to urbanization and suburban development brought about by the post-war boom, families like the Minogues were able to enjoy the conveniences of suburban living while still having access to Melbourne's thriving artistic and cultural scene. Anyone engaged in the arts, music, or movies was irresistibly drawn to the city. Kylie's interests started to take shape as a result of this dual existence—a suburban upbringing combined with exposure to a vibrant, artistic city. Being the oldest child in her family, Kylie's upbringing was characterized by her roles as an eager learner and a protective older sister. Her family placed a strong emphasis on responsibility, hard work, and valuing one's unique abilities. The dynamics in her home would have a big impact on Kylie's eventual quest for artistic discovery, originality, and popularity.

# The Influence of Her Parents and Siblings on Her Creative Development

The close-knit Minogue family greatly influenced Kylie's upbringing through the presence of her parents and siblings. The different origins of Kylie's parents, Ronald Charles Minogue and Carol Ann Jones, gave her a strong sense of equilibrium in life. Born in Wales, Carol Ann brought her love of the arts to her family after moving to Australia when she was a small child. Although her own time in the spotlight was brief, Carol's experience as a professional dancer gave her a deep understanding of the entertainment industry. Kylie gained a firsthand understanding of what it means to take one's creative goals seriously thanks to her experiences. It was impossible to deny Carol Ann's impact on her kids. From a young age, she exposed them to dance, music, and performance. Music from all genres and eras filled the house. Carol's dance training exposed her kids to rhythm, movement, and performance styles at a young age. Her mother's awareness of the pressures of the entertainment industry fostered Kylie's interest in these forms of artistic expression. Ronald, Kylie's father, on the other hand, provided consistency and common sense to the home. Ronald, who was an accountant and had a more practical outlook on life, frequently acted as a counterpoint to Carol's creative tendencies. Ronald's emphasis on education and making sure his kids were ready for life's obstacles gave Kylie the real-world experience she needed to handle the intricacies of the entertainment industry in her later years.

There were other Minogue kids with aspirations to pursue the arts besides Kylie. Brendan, born in 1970, and Dannii, born in 1971, were her siblings. Being the only son, Brendan decided to become a television cameraman. Despite taking a different route than his sisters, he helped the family get involved in the entertainment business. The youngest of the siblings, Dannii, would go on to establish herself as a successful singer and television personality. The Minogue family's sibling relationship was one of inspiration and support for one another. Growing up, Kylie and Dannii had a close sibling relationship and frequently performed together in casual settings or at local talent events. The two sisters' relationship was both cooperative and competitive, encouraging one another to take chances while offering consolation and support when things became tough. Although it came before Kylie's music career, Dannii's success in the entertainment business, especially in television in the early 1980s, surely boosted Kylie's self-esteem. Kylie's inventiveness thrived because of this family dynamic. Her father's practical approach and her mother's artistic sensibility gave her the drive to perform as well as the knowledge that success required hard work. Kylie was encouraged to follow her own path by her siblings, who offered her company and motivation.

## Childhood Interests and Early Artistic Inspirations

Kylie showed a broad range of artistic interests at an early age, many of which were fostered by her family. Dancing, music, and creative performances were valued in the Minogue home. When Kylie was still a young girl, Carol Ann enrolled her in dancing courses because of her own experiences as a performer. Early on, Kylie's innate ability to move was evident, and her passion for dancing grew. Ballet and contemporary dance particularly appealed to her since they taught her discipline, posture, and rhythm. Kylie loved dancing, but she was also enthralled with music. She had a varied musical foundation because her family was filled with the sounds of several genres, from pop to classical. The Minogue family regularly played music by artists like ABBA, Olivia Newton-John, and The Beatles, which had a big influence on Kylie's developing taste in music. It became evident that Kylie was growing her own ambitions for the stage as she appreciated how these artists could enthrall audiences with their music and charisma.

Local performances and school plays played a significant role in Kylie's early years. Her early exposure to dance and performance translated into a natural ability to command attention on stage, and she was frequently assigned to lead roles in school performances. Her abilities were immediately acknowledged by her teachers and peers, and Kylie's confidence increased with each performance. Kylie had opportunities to show her talents while attending Camberwell Primary School and then Camberwell High School. She was able to test her acting abilities through her participation in school shows, and she was able to develop her intellectual interests in an academic setting. In addition to her passion for performing, Kylie had a keen interest in literature and history, two topics that would subsequently have an unanticipated impact on her artistic output. Kylie's passion for acting started to develop when she was a teenager. Kylie made her television debut at the age of eleven in 1979, playing a minor part in the Australian drama series The Sullivans. Even though she had a little part, it was her first foray into the television industry and a taste of what was to come.

Future prospects in Australian television were made possible by this first encounter, and Kylie quickly expanded her involvement in the field. Kylie's participation in the Australian soap series Skyways in 1980 served to further solidify her early introduction to acting. Despite only being in her early teens, she immediately established a reputation for professionalism on set after receiving positive reviews for her performances. These early encounters exposed Kylie to the pressures of working in television and helped her hone her acting skills. However, Kylie's acting career didn't really take off until 1985, when she starred in The Henderson Kids. In a role that would make her a household figure in Australia, she portrayed the rebellious tomboy Charlene Mitchell. In addition to becoming well-liked by Australian viewers, her performance on the show caught the interest of business insiders, paving the way for her ultimate rise to fame in the music industry. The groundwork for Kylie's future international career was established by her early acting and performance experiences during her childhood. Her family and surroundings fostered her interest in dance, music, and acting, which equipped her with the skills necessary to thrive in a competitive field. Because of her early exposure and the influence of people closest to her, Kylie was already familiar with the difficulties of the entertainment industry by the time she reached adulthood.

# CHAPTER 2: KYLIE'S SCHOOLING DAYS

In addition to her artistic upbringing, Kylie Minogue's early years in Melbourne, Australia, were characterized by her academic pursuits. Kylie was initially exposed to the routine and structure of formal schooling at Camberwell Primary School, a nearby school in the Melbourne suburbs, where she was a young child. Kylie's school years, like those of many kids growing up in suburban Australia in the late 1960s and early 1970s, were a mix of social contacts, extracurricular activities, and academic learning that shaped her developing identity. Students and staff of Camberwell Primary School were part of a tiny, tight-knit community. Children might study and develop in a nurturing environment thanks to the surroundings. Kylie's enthusiasm to participate in school events and her lively personality were well-known among her peers. She showed a special interest in storytelling and the arts and performed exceptionally well in courses like English and history. She was praised frequently for her ability to pick up new ideas fast, and her teachers acknowledged her innate inventiveness and curiosity. Kylie also started to show off her early performance skills in elementary school. Her initial stage consisted of school plays and talent events, which gave her the chance to show off her developing skills to her teachers and peers. Early on, it was clear that she loved acting and performing, and these school productions gave her a stage on which to display her creative side. Students were encouraged to pursue creative endeavors in the educational setting, and Kylie enthusiastically seized these chances. Kylie remained steadfast in her academic pursuits even as her passion for the arts grew.

Regardless of Kylie's artistic aspirations, her parents, especially her father, Ronald Minogue, valued education and thought it was critical that she have a strong academic foundation. Ronald's influence made it possible for Kylie to stay focused on her studies while striking a balance between the demands of academic success and her developing passion for performance. Kylie was moving into a bigger, more varied school environment when she transferred to Camberwell High School in the early 1980s. Kylie had more options to follow her interests at Camberwell High School, which is renowned for its emphasis on creativity and intellectual excellence. While Kylie's academic prowess persisted, her love for the arts grew stronger. Kylie took part in a number of school performances, which helped her hone her acting and performance talents. The school featured a robust arts department. Kylie's years at Camberwell High School were crucial since it was during this time that she started to give a career in entertainment some serious thought. She was able to further develop her artistic abilities in the school's setting, which encouraged originality and self-expression. Even while Kylie remained committed to her academics, she realized that her future was on stage or screen and not in the classroom.

# Artistic Inclinations During Her School Years

As Kylie progressed through her scholastic years, her artistic tendencies became more apparent. She had always been interested in acting, dancing, and music, even as a small girl. At a young age, Kylie was exposed to the performing arts by her mother, Carol Ann, and her love for these activities had already started to develop by the time she started school. Kylie frequently played the lead in school plays and talent events while attending Camberwell Primary School. Learning lines, taking on roles, and performing in front of an audience were all things she cherished. Kylie soon established herself as one of the school's most gifted performers when her teachers saw how well she could draw in her peers during these performances. In addition to being enjoyable for Kylie, these early performances served as a valuable educational opportunity. She learned the self-control and commitment needed to succeed in the performing arts from them. Even as a young child, Kylie took her jobs seriously and addressed them professionally, learning her lines by heart. Even in these early years, her dedication to her work was clear. Kylie continued to be heavily involved in artistic endeavors after she transferred to Cameron High School. She was able to hone her acting, dancing, and music abilities thanks to the school's extensive arts curriculum. As a frequent participant in the school's theatrical performances, Kylie continued to hone her acting skills by taking on increasingly difficult roles. Kylie was drawn to dancing in addition to acting. Her passion for movement became a significant component of her artistic expression as she began taking dance lessons outside of school at an early age.

Kylie frequently included dancing in her school presentations, which gave her stage appearance an additional dimension of energy. Kylie stood out from her friends due to her ability to blend dancing and acting, and it became evident that she had a natural knack for performing. Kylie's school years were also significantly impacted by music. Music had always permeated the Minogue home, and Kylie's exposure to a variety of genres shaped her own taste in music. Kylie took part in music classes at school and worked on her voice skills. Even though Kylie would go on to become well-known for her pop career, her musical abilities were still in their infancy while she was a student. She occasionally participated in modest musical numbers during school musicals and sang in school choirs. But formal performances weren't the only thing she was drawn to. In the course of her regular school life, Kylie was also well-known for her inventiveness. Kylie was always willing to provide her artistic vision to any endeavor, whether it was creating costumes for school productions or assisting with stage direction. She soon established herself as a key player in the school's creative community, and her professors and classmates frequently looked to her for artistic advice.

# The Balance of Schoolwork and Emerging Career Ambitions

Kylie had the difficulty of juggling her academic obligations with her developing professional goals as her artistic abilities continued to grow. Kylie had already begun to receive some recognition for her acting skills by the time she was in high school, especially because of her early TV roles in programs like Skyways and The Sullivans. Despite the excitement of these chances, Kylie had to carefully manage her time to avoid sacrificing her academic performance. Kylie's parents were very helpful in assisting her in keeping this equilibrium. Even when Kylie's acting career started to take off, Carol Ann and Ronald, who both valued education, urged her to put her studies first. Carol saw the necessity for Kylie to have a well-rounded education while also understanding the demands of the entertainment industry, having worked in the performing arts herself. Regardless of Kylie's job goals, Ronald, being the practical one, demanded that she finish her education. For her part, Kylie was committed to being successful in both fields. She put a lot of effort into keeping up with her coursework, frequently finishing homework and preparing for tests in between acting engagements. Although juggling the responsibilities of education and her expanding career in entertainment wasn't always simple, Kylie was able to do so because of her work ethic and discipline. Kylie's job goals became more clear during her high school years. She was certain that she wanted to work in the performing arts, and her school experiences only confirmed this desire.

Her early television roles and participation in school performances gave her the courage to pursue a career in acting and singing. But Kylie also recognized the value of a strong educational foundation, and she was determined to complete her degree. Kylie was cast in the television series The Henderson Kids in 1985 while she was still a student at Camberwell High School. This was a pivotal moment in her career because it signaled the change from minor, one-off parts to a larger role in a popular series. Positive reviews were given to Kylie's performance on The Henderson Kids, which gave her the opportunity to show off her acting skills to a wider audience. Kylie stayed dedicated to her studies in spite of the responsibilities of her position on The Henderson Kids. While filming the series, she kept going to school, frequently balancing her academic obligations with lengthy hours on set. During this time in her life, she had to strike a careful balance between her desire to pursue a career and her obligation to finish her education. In the middle of the 1980s, Kylie graduated from Camberwell High School, having finally finished her high school education. Although Kylie had already established herself in the Australian entertainment industry by the time she graduated, her education continued to play a significant role in her growth. Her ability to manage her academic obligations and professional goals showed her commitment and self-control, traits that will benefit her in the future. Kylie's school years were a pivotal time in her life since they gave her the intellectual groundwork and artistic chances that would influence her future. Her career as a globally recognized performer would be greatly influenced by the lessons she gained during these years, both in the classroom and on stage.

# CHAPTER 3: STEPPING INTO THE SPOTLIGHT: EARLY ACTING CAREER

Kylie Minogue started her career in acting and television at an early age, which would ultimately lead to her becoming a global celebrity. Her early aspirations were inspired by the artistic atmosphere around her. Kylie had already decided she wanted to pursue a career in entertainment by the time she was a teenager. But rather than a quick ascent to stardom, her initial acting career consisted of a string of modest but important parts that laid the groundwork for her subsequent achievements. When Kylie was eleven years old in 1979, she made her television debut on the well-liked Australian drama series The Sullivans, which was set in World War II. The program, which focused on the life of the Sullivan family and their experiences throughout the war, was a mainstay of Australian television from 1976 to 1983. Despite having a minor role, Kylie's debut into the professional acting industry was significant. Although she had a little role, the experience gave her an early insight into the television industry and helped her become acquainted with its workings. For Kylie, The Sullivans was a significant turning point since it gave her insight into the inner workings of a popular television program. Kylie gained knowledge about the rigors of the set, the value of learning lines, and the self-control needed to remain professional in front of the camera there. The experience helped her build the fundamental abilities that will aid her in the future while she was still a young girl.

Kylie's next noteworthy role after appearing on The Sullivans was in the 1980 television series Skyways. The daily operations of an airport were the focus of the Australian drama series Skyways, which combined the protagonists' personal and professional lives. Once more, Kylie's contribution was quite small, but it helped her resume grow and gave her more exposure to the TV business. Although it was a brief role, Kylie's portrayal of Carla in a few episodes gave her developing acting career a new angle. Even though Kylie's television career was still extremely young at this point, her roles showed how dedicated she was to acting. Both Skyways and The

Sullivans gave Kylie an idea of what an acting career would entail, and although these early roles did not immediately propel her to prominence, they were crucial in helping her hone her skills. These experiences were crucial because they prepared her for bigger chances while exposing her to the rigors and realities of acting. Kylie was still going to school and juggling her academic obligations while continuing to play these supporting parts. By this point, it was evident that acting was a passion she was committed to pursue seriously rather than merely a passing curiosity. Kylie's innate charm and her expanding understanding of the television business put her on the path to greater possibilities.

## Breakthrough Role in Neighbours (1986) as Charlene Robinson

When Kylie was cast in the Australian serial opera Neighbours in 1986, it was her real television debut and would forever alter the course of her career. Since its 1985 premiere, Neighbours has been one of Australia's most watched soap operas. Its realistic plots center on the lives of families in the made-up Melbourne suburb of Erinsborough. Kylie was chosen to play Charlene Robinson, a lively, tomboyish mechanic who struck a chord with viewers right away. At the time, Charlene stood out from the other characters on Australian television. She distinguished herself as a new, genuine character with her grounded demeanor and uncompromising outlook. Kylie's performance as Charlene was ideal for the part and gave her a greater opportunity than ever to demonstrate her innate acting skills. Charlene made a spectacular entry into Neighbors. Her character made her debut in a notable episode where she scales the window of Scott Robinson's Ramsay Street house.

Jason Donovan, who would later play Kylie's co-star and romantic interest both on and off screen, plays Scott Robinson. Viewers were immediately drawn in by this memorable opening, and Charlene quickly became a favorite. Viewers immediately identified with Kylie's portrayal of Charlene as a strong-willed, rebellious young lady who wasn't afraid to defend herself. Millions of people were enthralled by Charlene's turbulent romance with Scott Robinson, which was the focus of her Neighbors plot. The on-screen romance between Kylie and Jason Donovan became one of the most talked-about elements of the show because of their unquestionable connection. Specifically, the July 1987 broadcast of Charlene and Scott's wedding episode turned into one of the most memorable events in Australian television history. With over 20 million viewers tuning in to witness the couple's wedding, Kylie became a household name in both Australia and the UK, where Neighbours had a considerable fan base. Kylie's portrayal of Charlene and the success of Neighbors made her a household name. Her fame skyrocketed in the UK, where Neighbours was a mainstay of daytime television, and she became a national figure in Australia. Kylie's portrayal of Charlene Robinson helped define a period in Australian television, and she went beyond simply being a character to become a cultural phenomenon. The position gave Kylie the exposure and acknowledgment she required to advance her career. Kylie received praise from critics for her portrayal of Charlene as Neighbours dominated the airwaves. Her influence on the Australian entertainment industry was demonstrated in 1987 when she was awarded the Logie Award for Most Popular Actress. Kylie had gone from being a young actress playing supporting parts to becoming one of the most adored celebrities on Australian television, so the recognition was well-earned.

## The Impact of Neighbours on Her Early Popularity

It is impossible to overestimate the influence of Neighbors on Kylie Minogue's early success. The show was a cultural powerhouse, especially in Australia and the UK, where millions of people watched it every day. Many of the show's most cherished plots revolved around Kylie's character, Charlene, and her portrayal cemented her status as one of the most promising young actors of the era. Fans of all ages in Australia loved Kylie. Viewers were moved by Charlene's likable hardships, tenacity, and lively attitude, especially young ladies who looked up to her. Because of her innate warmth and genuineness, Kylie became a favorite right away, and her fame spread beyond Neighbors. Her reputation as a national superstar was cemented when the media started to take notice of her and frequently featured her face on magazine and tabloid covers. But neighbors' influence extended beyond Australia. In the United Kingdom, where it was aired during the day, the show gained popularity and a devoted fan base. One of the most viewed TV shows in the UK was Neighbours, and Kylie's portrayal of Charlene contributed to the show's record-breaking success. In the UK, Kylie's fan base increased rapidly, and she became well-known throughout the nation.

Because of Neighbours' worldwide fame, Kylie was able to start a career outside of acting. Even though she was still concentrating on her part in the performance, the publicity she got allowed her to enter the music business, where she would soon have an even greater influence. She subsequently pursued a career in music as a result of the exposure and renown she received from her time on Neighbours, which gave her the drive to take on new challenges and chances. It is noteworthy that Kylie's success throughout her tenure on Neighbours was a combination of her own ability and hard work, as well as the popularity of the show. A major contributor to Kylie's success was her ability to depict Charlene as a lively and approachable figure. She brought Charlene to life in a way that audiences found incredibly compelling. Her tenure on Neighbours is still regarded as one of the most iconic eras of her career, and it served as the basis for her subsequent achievements in acting and music. Even as Kylie got ready to switch from TV to music, her time on Neighbours continued to play a significant role in who she was. In addition to introducing her to millions of admirers worldwide, the show had allowed her to hone her acting and performance abilities. The foundation for Kylie's subsequent journey—one that would soon make her one of the biggest pop sensations of her generation—was laid by her early acting career, especially her stint on Neighbours.

# CHAPTER 4: THE LEAP INTO MUSIC

Kylie Minogue's rise from TV personality to music icon happened as quickly as it did well. Because of her role as Charlene Robinson on Neighbours, she was already well-known in Australia and the UK by the middle of the 1980s. But Kylie's drive and passion to push herself artistically went well beyond acting. Her career would eventually be defined by her foray into music, which catapulted her to international renown. She established herself as a pop icon with the publication of her first album Kylie in 1988 and her first song, "The Loco-Motion," paving the way for a long career in the music business. With the release of the single "The Loco Motion," a rendition of the 1962 hit originally performed by Little Eva, Kylie Minogue made her professional music industry debut in July 1987. The single's release has a slightly coincidental backstory. Executives from the Australian record label Mushroom Records were drawn to Kylie's performance of "The Loco-Motion" on stage at a Neighbors cast party. Kylie's music career started to take form after they swiftly signed her after realizing her talent as a vocalist. Local producer Mike Duffy produced "The Locomotion," which was recorded in Melbourne. Initially, there was some uncertainty about the success of an actress-turned-singer, but those reservations were quickly dispelled. When "The Loco-Motion" was released in July 1987, it immediately became popular in Australia and topped the charts for an astounding seven weeks. That year, it was Australia's best-selling single, and the song's tremendous popularity showed that Kylie's musical endeavors were much more than a passing fad. The public was captivated by her lively, upbeat rendition of the song and her indisputable charm. Kylie's version of "The Loco-Motion" was contagious, combining her own distinct appeal with the essence of the original. From teens to older fans who were familiar with the 1960s original, the lively tempo, catchy chorus, and nostalgic charm struck a chord with a wide range of listeners.

In addition to being widely played on the radio, the song was also frequently featured on music video shows, which increased Kylie's visibility. Through Neighbours, she had already made a name for herself, and the popularity of her debut single showed that she could transition from television to music. Kylie's worldwide breakthrough was made possible by the popularity of "The Locomotion" in Australia. It was decided to take Kylie's music career to a wider audience once Mushroom Records realized they had something unique in her. At this point, her career path took an even more dramatic shift when the song attracted the attention of British producers Stock Aitken Waterman, a trio that helped produce some of the 1980s' biggest pop songs.

## Signing with Mushroom Records and Working with Stock Aitken Waterman

Kylie had achieved national success with "The Loco-Motion" thanks to Mushroom Records, but they realized she needed to collaborate with seasoned producers who could create singles for the international market if she wanted to advance her career. The British songwriting and production team Stock Aitken Waterman, which consists of Pete Waterman, Matt Aitken, and Mike Stock, is introduced. By 1987, Stock

Aitken Waterman (SAW) had already made a name for themselves as hitmakers, with singles that reached the top of the charts for singers such as Rick Astley, Dead or Alive, and Bananarama. The collaboration that would result in some of Kylie's most famous songs began when she went to London to collaborate with SAW in late 1987. "I Should Be So Lucky," which would go on to become a huge hit, was the first song she recorded with the group. Kylie and SAW were a natural fit because of their shared ability to write catchy, radio-friendly pop tunes, as well as Kylie's unique voice and popular status. Kylie subsequently said that although her first encounter with the three was short, the group promptly set to work on the song, finishing it in a matter of hours. "I Should Be So Lucky," which was released in December 1987 in the UK and February 1988 in Australia, changed Kylie's life.

Several nations, including the UK, Australia, Germany, and Japan, had the song at the top of their charts. For five weeks, it remained at the top of the UK charts, solidifying Kylie's place as a legitimate pop star. "I Should Be So Lucky" served as Kylie's ideal entrance to the world of music. The song became a mainstay of 1980s pop music thanks to its catchy tune and lighthearted lyrics. Kylie formally signed a long-term contract with PWL Records, a division of Mushroom Records in the UK, following the success of "I Should Be So Lucky," guaranteeing that she would continue to collaborate with SAW on upcoming songs. With the help of PWL Records' global reach and Stock Aitken Waterman's experience, Kylie became a growing celebrity not just in Australia and the UK but also globally. The release of a full-length album was the next obvious step since it was evident that Kylie's music career was no longer a side endeavor but rather her primary priority.

## Release of Her Debut Album Kylie (1988) and Its Worldwide Impact

Kylie Minogue's first studio album, simply called Kylie, was released on July 4, 1988. The energetic dance-pop songs on the album, which was produced by Stock Aitken Waterman, highlighted Kylie's vocal prowess and solidified her status as a pop sensation. Hit songs from the album, such as "The Loco-Motion," "I Should Be So Lucky," and "Got to Be Certain," all helped to fuel its enormous economic success. When Kylie was first released, it became an instant smash in Australia and other countries. The album spent six weeks in a row at the top of the UK Albums Chart after its debut. It peaked at number two on the charts in Australia, enhancing Kylie's reputation as one of the most popular musicians in that nation. Kylie was a commercial success in Europe, Asia, and even the United States, where it peaked at number 53 on the Billboard 200. It also topped the charts in the UK and Australia. There was no denying Kylie's global influence. The album became one of the best-selling albums of the late 1980s after selling over five million copies worldwide. It received six platinum certifications in the UK and four platinum certifications in Australia. These sales numbers demonstrated Kylie's global appeal since her music crossed national boundaries and connected with listeners everywhere. Kylie's triumph signaled a sea change in her career, demonstrating that she was a genuine pop phenomenon with global appeal rather than just a TV actress with a few successful songs. Kylie's singles were a major factor in the album's popularity. In May 1988, the album's third single, "Got to Be Certain," peaked at number one in Australia and made it into the UK's top five. Kylie's winning streak was maintained with the release of her fourth song, "Je Ne Sais Pas Pourquoi," in October 1988. It peaked at number two in the UK and made it into the top 20 in Australia. In addition to its sales and chart success, Kylie signaled the start of Kylie Minogue's artistic development. The album highlighted Kylie's potential to develop as a vocalist and recording artist despite being based on the lively, dance-pop style for which Stock Aitken Waterman was famous. Although at first thought to be delicate and girlish, her voice—which combines delicacy with a faint sense of strength and resolve—became one of the characteristics that set her music apart. Kylie's public image was significantly impacted by her release as well. Kylie Minogue's vivid personality and daring, colorful attire made her a style icon for young ladies in the late 1980s. Fans were drawn to her because of her sense of style, self-assurance, and amiable personality, in addition to her singing. Because of her ability to relate to her fans personally, Kylie became more than simply a pop artist; her followers could look up to and respect her. Additionally, Kylie showed that she could adjust to the constantly shifting pop music landscape. Kylie was well-positioned to be at the forefront of the industry as the 1980s came to an end and musical preferences started to change. She had a strong foundation thanks to her work with Stock Aitken Waterman, but she was also excited to try out new sounds and approaches in the years to come.

Kylie's triumph signaled the start of a career in the music industry that would last for decades. Kylie had solidified her status as one of the biggest pop artists of the 1980s by the end of the album's promotional cycle, and she was prepared to keep gaining ground. Although it had been a calculated risk, the foray into music paid off in ways that no one could have predicted. From a soap opera actress to a worldwide pop sensation, Kylie Minogue's career was only getting started.

# CHAPTER 5: GLOBAL STARDOM AND POP SUCCESS

Kylie Minogue had solidified her position as one of the most promising new artists in the pop music industry by the end of the 1980s. She had gone quickly from being a television actress to becoming a pop sensation, and she had no intention of stopping down. She was already on her way to becoming a worldwide celebrity following the incredible success of her 1988 debut album, Kylie. She cemented her status as a global pop icon in 1989 with the release of her second album, Enjoy Yourself. But being famous came with its own set of difficulties, and Kylie had to manage the demands of the limelight while gaining a large following around the world and continuing to be at the top of the charts. 1988 was a significant year for Kylie Minogue. With tracks like "I Should Be So Lucky" and "The Loco-Motion," her debut album Kylie, which was produced by the British hitmaking company Stock Aitken Waterman (SAW), topped the charts and made her a global celebrity. The album sold millions of copies worldwide and peaked at the top of several charts, including those in Australia and the United Kingdom. Kylie, however, wasn't satisfied with sitting on her laurels. Enjoy Yourself, her second studio album, was already in the works by the end of 1988 and was scheduled for release in October 1989. Kylie wanted to show her development as an artist and capitalize on the popularity of her debut with Enjoy Yourself. She worked with Stock Aitken Waterman, who had written her earlier singles, once more, and the outcome was another set of snappy, danceable pop tunes that were popular with a broad audience. When "Hand on Your Heart," the lead single, was released in April 1989, it immediately became an enormous hit. It became Kylie's third UK chart-topping song in less than a year when it peaked at number one on the UK Singles Chart. The song's catchy tune, lively production, and lyrics about love and resiliency were all excellent examples of the SAW formula in action. With her self-assured and captivating performance on the song, Kylie cemented her place as a major pop star. The album's second single, "Wouldn't Change a Thing," was released in July 1989 after the success of "Hand on Your Heart." With a peak position of number two on the UK Singles Chart, the song extended Kylie's run of top ten hits. Similar to its predecessor, "Wouldn't Change a Thing" was a cheerful pop anthem that demonstrated Kylie's charisma as a vocalist and her talent for creating uplifting music. It did well abroad as well, placing in the top ten in Finland, Ireland, and Australia. The popularity of these singles contributed to the excitement surrounding the October 1989 release of Enjoy Yourself. Kylie's album Enjoy Yourself became the second straight album to debut at the top of the UK Albums Chart. The album's commercial success was remarkable; it was awarded double platinum in Australia and four times platinum in the UK, proving that Kylie's appeal was genuinely worldwide. The album's blend of dance-pop and ballads gave Kylie the chance to demonstrate her range as a performer.

Fan favorites like "Never Too Late" and "Tears on My Pillow" were added to her expanding hit list. Released as the fourth single from Enjoy Yourself, "Tears on My Pillow" stood out for its nostalgic vibe. It featured a distinct side of Kylie, paying homage to old pop while keeping a modern edge. It was a rendition of the 1958 song by Little Anthony and the Imperials. In January 1990, the song peaked at number one in the UK, giving Kylie another number-one single. It also showed that she could take previous songs and turn them into her own, which was a talent that would help her in her career. In addition to putting out two successful albums by the end of 1989, Kylie solidified her status as one of the most well-liked female pop stars worldwide. Her popularity kept rising thanks to her run of number-one singles and steady media appearances. However, popularity also brought with it more pressure, and Kylie had to deal with the responsibilities of a career that was growing quickly on a global basis.

# International Tours and Building a Global Fanbase

In 1989, Kylie started her first concert tour, which was appropriately called the Disco in Dream tour, as her music career proceeded to take off. The tour was a pivotal moment in her career since it gave her the chance to interact with her audience live and enhance her reputation as a performer. Even though she had already established herself as a successful recording artist, touring gave her the chance to interact more deeply with her fans and demonstrate her live skills. As part of the Disco in Dream tour, Kylie visited locations in the UK and Asia, notably Japan, where she already had a sizable fan base. Kylie found that Japan was a particularly important market, and her performances there were overwhelmingly well received. Kylie's ability to enthrall audiences across several nations proved how broad her appeal is. Her songs struck a chord with listeners whether in Europe, Australia, or Asia, and her live appearances solidified her reputation as a worldwide pop sensation. During this time, Kylie's live performances were distinguished by their vibrant stage designs, exuberant dancing, and her indisputable charm. At first, several reviewers doubted Kylie's ability to control a stage, but she soon showed that she was more than capable of putting on exciting and captivating performances.

Her early tours demonstrated her commitment and will to be a successful live singer, even though they lacked the lavish production values that would eventually characterize her performances. Her reach was further extended in 1990 with the Enjoy Yourself tour, which followed the success of the Disco in Dream tour. During this tour, Kylie performed in bigger venues throughout Europe and Australia. With sold-out performances and fervent audiences at every stop, the tour was again another critical and financial triumph. Kylie saw traveling as an opportunity to build enduring relationships with her fans rather than merely marketing her albums. One of the main reasons she developed a devoted following that would stick by her throughout her career was her ability to interact with her audience live. Additionally, Kylie's foreign tours helped her become more well-known in nations where she had not previously had as much fame. For instance, Kylie's debut album and "The Loco-Motion" had both seen moderate popularity in the US, but her later albums had not had the same degree of commercial success. Even though mainstream chart success was still elusive at this point in her career, her US tours and promotional activities helped her cultivate a devoted fan base. Kylie's ability to stay in close contact with her fans, no matter where they were from, was one of the most important factors in her ascent to international fame. Kylie's friendly and grounded demeanor won over fans whether she was playing in Australia, the UK, or Japan. She was frequently characterized as approachable and modest, traits that appealed to fans who perceived her as someone who had maintained her sense of reality in spite of her rising stardom. One of the hallmarks of her work and a factor in maintaining her appeal over the years would be her relationship with her fan base.

# Dealing with the Pressures of Overnight Fame

The pressures of being a worldwide superstar were something Kylie Minogue struggled with as her career grew. She had already experienced a quick ascent to prominence by the time Enjoy Yourself was released, but her unexpected success came with its own set of difficulties. As Kylie's schedule grew more demanding and the media's interest in her personal life increased, she found it more and more difficult to balance the demands of her work with her personal life. Kylie had to deal with the heavy media attention that accompanied her celebrity status from an early age. Following her breakthrough performance in Neighbours and the popularity of her first album, the media became enthralled with every facet of her life, including her relationships and style choices. Particularly persistent in their coverage of Kylie, the tabloids frequently sensationalized her private life. Kylie's friendship with fellow Neighbors star Jason Donovan was one of the most well-known features of her early notoriety.

Audiences had been enthralled by the couple's on-screen romance as Scott and Charlene, and the media's fixation on Kylie was only heightened when their real-life relationship was made public.

Kylie admitted that she finds it difficult to handle the demands of celebrity at such a young age as a result of the media's continual attention. She discussed the challenges of being in the spotlight and how it affected her personal life in interviews. Despite the difficulties, Kylie maintained her composure and professionalism, not allowing the media's interference to ruin her career. Her perseverance and work ethic were demonstrated by her capacity to remain normal despite her tremendous celebrity. Kylie had to contend with the demands of continuously establishing herself as an artist as her career developed. Despite her enormous economic success, several reviewers still saw her as a manufactured pop singer who was produced by the Stock Aitken Waterman team. Knowing these comments, Kylie started to consider how she could develop as an artist and get greater creative control over her songs, even though she still loved her collaboration with SAW. There was a lot of pressure on Kylie to maintain her fame and develop as an artist, but she met these obstacles head-on. She persisted in putting in endless hours of work, juggling promotional appearances, recording sessions, and tours while juggling the demands of celebrity. One of her career's defining characteristics would be her ability to manage these demands with professionalism and grace, which let her weather the highs and lows of the music business and hold onto her position as a worldwide pop icon.

# CHAPTER 6: EVOLVING AS AN ARTIST

Kylie Minogue was about to undergo a major artistic metamorphosis as the 1990s progressed. She was solidly established as a worldwide pop artist by the explosive ascent to popularity that defined her career in the late 1980s. But Kylie was keen to reinvent herself, letting go of the "girl next door" persona that had been developed during her formative musical years. Kylie underwent a significant development at this time, both vocally and aesthetically. Released on November 12, 1990, Rhythm of Love marked a significant turning point in Kylie's development into a more mature, self-assured artist and performer. With Rhythm of Love, Kylie Minogue took a daring turn from the sweet pop tunes that characterized her first two albums. Kylie and the British songwriting and production team Stock Aitken Waterman (SAW) collaborated on the album, which was released by PWL (Pete Waterman Entertainment). For this album, Kylie continued to work with SAW as a professional, but it was becoming more obvious that she was taking greater control of her image and sound. The album demonstrated

Kylie's wish to explore themes of love, grief, and desire in a more sophisticated and mature manner than her prior work, in addition to reflecting the increasing impact of club culture and dance music. The album became one of her most successful albums to date, debuting at number nine in the UK Albums Chart. In the UK and Australia, it received platinum certification, which increased Kylie's marketability.

Critics' reactions were mostly favorable, with many praising her development as a recording artist and her calculated choice to explore more modern dance-pop territory. This change in tone was crucial to Kylie's development. With elements of house and synth-driven beats that were popular in clubs at the time, the album perfectly captured the spirit of dance music of the 1990s. Kylie was able to stay relevant in the quickly evolving music industry because of songs like "What Do I Have to Do" and "Shocked," which featured a dance-pop feel that was very contemporary. Kylie's increasing engagement in the creative process was demonstrated by the fact that Rhythm of Love was her first album to include songwriting contributions. She was starting to develop a more complex artistic personality rather than just being a puppet of the industry. Her literary contributions, which also marked a change in her storytelling, offered intimate perspectives on independence, relationships, and love.

## Classic Songs: "Better the Devil You Know"

"Better the Devil You Know," the album's debut single released in April 1990, is arguably the most famous song from Rhythm of Love. The song swiftly marked a turning point in Kylie's career, signifying her evolution from a youthful pop sensation to a more nuanced and complicated performer. "Better the Devil You Know" was a huge commercial triumph. The British Phonographic Industry (BPI) certified it gold, and it peaked at number two on the UK Singles Chart. The song's catchy chorus and throbbing dance beats made it an instant hit in clubs, and its fusion of pop and house influences made it suitable for a larger audience. Reaching number four on the Australian singles charts, the track's performance in Australia was as noteworthy.

But "Better the Devil You Know" had more to its impact than just its musical arrangement. Paul Goldman's accompanying music video played a crucial role in influencing how the general public saw Kylie. The naive picture from her previous work was gone. Kylie seemed more glitzy and confident in the video, dancing in a nightclub while wearing bolder attire. With its more risqué and flirty visuals, the video signaled a bolder approach to her craft and signified a considerable break from her previous visual style.

The song itself also came to represent Kylie's friendship with INXS lead singer Michael Hutchence. At the time of their highly publicized relationship, Kylie and Hutchence were rumored to have pushed Kylie to embrace a more daring side in both her music and her persona. Their relationship came at a crucial time in Kylie's personal life, coinciding with her development as an artist. The words of the song alluded to fortitude and self-determination. "Better the Devil You Know" was an allegory for Kylie's connection with her career, even though it was initially about the difficulties of personal relationships. She had mastered the skill of navigating the demands of celebrity, striking a balance between her ambition to develop as an artist and the demands of the industry and her admirers. One of Kylie's most enduring and well-loved songs, "Better the Devil You Know," signaled the start of her path toward artistic freedom.

## Experimenting with Her Image and Sound in the Early 1990s

Kylie Minogue embraced a phase of artistic experimentation as the 1990s went on, questioning the stereotypes of what a pop star ought to be. Her early success had been predicated on a meticulously maintained façade of sweetness and innocence, but as she grew older, she also felt the need to transcend those limitations. This creative experimentation was evident in the music on Rhythm of Love. Songs like "Step Back in Time," which was the album's second single and released in October 1990, and "Shocked," which was the album's fourth single, demonstrated a significant shift from her previous work. The dance and house music elements that were becoming noticeable in her sound were reflected in both songs. With its catchy groove and vintage production, "Step Back in Time" was a nostalgic homage to the disco era, while "Shocked" symbolized Kylie's growing courage to take chances both musically and artistically. Kylie experimented with more than just her music. Additionally, she started to reimagine herself in ways that were far more controversial than what audiences had previously witnessed. Her fashion choices became more daring, and she frequently collaborated with renowned designers like Dolce & Gabbana and Jean-Paul Gaultier to create a look that was both daring and elegant. Through these partnerships, she was able to establish herself as a style icon in addition to her pop star status by aligning herself with the world of high fashion. The May 1991 release of "Shocked" is among the most illustrative instances of her artistic development. The British dance production duo DNA remixed the record, giving it a more intense house sound and bringing Kylie even closer to the emerging club culture of the era. Her increasing self-assurance was bolstered by the music video for "Shocked," which showed her as a strong performer at the top of her game. Kylie's status as a pop pioneer who isn't afraid to embrace new trends and push the boundaries of her image was cemented by the mix of her futuristic look, high-end clothing, and choreography. There were difficulties throughout this time of reinvention. Some sections of the press criticized Kylie when she started to exercise more creative freedom because they couldn't seem to connect her new persona with the endearing pop sensation they had known. Whether Kylie could continue to be successful commercially while taking a more experimental approach was questioned.

Nevertheless, Kylie persisted in her resolve to develop and demonstrate that she was more than a manufactured pop sensation. Her image was directly impacted by the changes occurring in her personal life as well. As previously said, she was greatly impacted by her friendship with Michael Hutchence. Kylie was greatly influenced by Hutchence, who was well-known for his rebellious and rock star persona, to embrace a more daring side of herself on a personal and professional level. Even though their relationship was brief, it had a significant influence on Kylie's artistic development, especially in the early 1990s.

# CHAPTER 7: BREAKING THE MOLD: THE 1990s TRANSFORMATION

For Kylie Minogue, the 1990s was a significant phase of reinvention during which she attempted to reinterpret her identity on a personal and musical level. She was labeled a manufactured celebrity after her early success in the late 1980s, which was primarily based on her pop image and a cooperation with Stock Aitken Waterman (SAW). Despite the fact that this time had produced successes that solidified her status as a global pop sensation, Kylie was keen to escape the limitations that accompanied this affiliation. Her deliberate departure from the bubblegum pop sound that had defined her early years and her development into a more complex and well-regarded musician occurred in the 1990s. The working relationship between Kylie Minogue and Stock Aitken Waterman (SAW) had started to show indications of tension by the early 1990s. Even though the group had a number of singles that reached the top of the charts, Kylie was becoming more and more interested in taking more creative control of her music. She felt constrained by the inflexible structure that SAW had put in place around her, and she had grown as a person and an artist. Both musically and in terms of her reputation, she was now constrained by the bubblegum pop sound that had been so popular. She was growing increasingly frustrated with the lack of artistic control. A significant change occurred during the recording of her fourth studio album, Let's Get to It, which was released in October 1991. Kylie's influence was more apparent even though SAW still produced the record. She co-wrote a number of the album's songs, such as "Live and Learn" and "Right Here, Right Now." These songs had a more refined and mature tone than her earlier work, even if they were still in the pop genre. Let's Get to It, however, fell short of her previous albums' level of economic success despite this endeavor to herald change.

Compared to her previous three albums, it was a relative letdown, peaking at number 15 on the UK Albums Chart. Both fans and critics felt that Kylie was starting to outgrow her collaboration with SAW. The last straw occurred when two new songs, "What Kind of Fool

(Heard All That Before)" and "Celebration," were recorded for her 1992 Greatest Hits compilation album. Even though these songs did fairly well on the charts, Kylie was no longer as excited about the project. The formulaic pop songs that SAW had been creating for her no longer satisfied her. Kylie made the crucial choice to split from Stock Aitken Waterman and their company PWL in 1992. She didn't make this choice lightly because the partnership had really benefited her. But it was obvious that Kylie needed to accept new influences and escape the limitations of her background if she was to develop as an artist. A new era began when she left SAW, one in which she would actively direct her career according to her own wishes.

## The Critical Success of Kylie Minogue (1994)

Following her 1992 departure from Stock Aitken Waterman, Kylie had to rebuild her career without the group that had made her a global celebrity. It was both necessary and risky because Kylie wanted to establish herself as a multifaceted and deep artist. She agreed to a contract with Deconstruction Records, a label renowned for its lineup of more avant-garde and experimental musicians. Her wish to take her music down a more complex path was evident from this. Kylie Minogue, her fifth studio album, was released in September 1994. Compared to her earlier work, it was a significant change.

The album, which was produced by producers Steve Anderson and Brothers in Rhythm, saw Kylie take on a more sophisticated, adult-oriented sound. It combined pop, dance, and house music components with more thoughtful and intimate lyrics. The frothy, shallow tracks that had once characterized her were no longer there. Songs that demonstrated a greater level of emotional maturity took their place. Released in August 1994, the album's debut song, "Confide in Me," was a forceful declaration of intent. With its ethereal melody and sweeping strings, the song marked Kylie's break from her earlier sound. Her vocal range was displayed in a more dramatic and expressive setting, which was unlike anything she had ever done. "Confide in Me" peaked at number one in Australia and number two on the UK Singles Chart, demonstrating Kylie's ability to stay relevant even after her musical approach had changed. In contrast to her previous pop singles, the song's lyrics, which addressed issues of trust and vulnerability, struck a chord with listeners. It was obvious that Kylie was now an independent artist and was not happy to be labeled as a manufactured pop star. "Put Yourself in My Place" and "Where Is the Feeling?" were two more standout singles from the album that continued Kylie Minogue's introduction of an elegant pop aesthetic. The majority of critics gave Kylie positive reviews, lauding her for her courage in changing who she was and for creating an album that seemed genuine and represented her development as a person. With a debut at number four on the UK Albums Chart and platinum status in Australia, Kylie Minogue's album was a commercial triumph. More significantly, it brought Kylie the critical respect she had never had before. Her ability to overcome the constraints of her early career was solidified by the album's popularity, which also established her as a more reputable and long-lasting personality in the pop music industry. Additionally, it set the stage for the artistic risks she would take with Impossible Princess, her following album.

## Exploring Indie-Pop with Impossible Princess (1997)

The release of Impossible Princess in 1997 marked the pinnacle of Kylie Minogue's metamorphosis. With this album, Kylie made a bold and drastic change, fully embracing alternative and indie-pop influences. For Kylie, the mid-1990s marked a time of intense artistic and emotional discovery. She had gotten heavily active in the London art scene after leaving SAW, and she had been exposed to a greater variety of musical styles, such as rock, electronica, and trip-hop. Her future project would be influenced by these factors. The October 22, 1997, release of Impossible Princess was greatly impacted by Kylie's connection to French photographer Stéphane Sednaoui, who had exposed her to a more avant-garde environment. The album's title, which was later renamed simply Kylie Minogue in some regions following Princess Diana's untimely death in August 1997, reflected Kylie's struggle to balance her personal goals with her public persona. Kylie co-wrote every song on the album, playing a major part in both its writing and production for the first time in her career. This was a daring step that demonstrated her developing self-assurance as an artist.

Kylie has never recorded anything like the sound of Impossible Princess before. With reflective and occasionally personal lyrics, the album combined dance, electronica, and indie-pop influences. Songs like "Some Kind of Bliss," which Kylie co-wrote with Manic Street Preachers members James Dean Bradfield and Sean Moore, demonstrated her newfound passion for rock music, while "Breathe" had a strong trip-hop influence. Identity, self-discovery, and loneliness were all topics covered in Impossible Princess's songs. As a prominent celebrity and a woman in her late 20s, Kylie had been struggling with her place in the world for the past few years, and the album's material exposed these issues. It was quite intimate, with Kylie musing on her relationships, career, and life in a way that was unusual for a pop singer of her caliber. Impossible Princess received mixed reviews when it was first released, despite its artistic brilliance. Some of Kylie's more popular fans were turned off by the album's avant-garde style, and its sales performance paled in comparison to her earlier albums. The album didn't do well in the UK, peaking at number 10 on the charts. But it did better in Australia, where it was certified platinum and peaked at number four on the ARIA Albums Chart. Impossible Princess has been reassessed by both fans and reviewers over time, and it is currently regarded as one of Kylie's most daring and significant works. Despite being a commercial failure at first, the album was a turning point in Kylie's career since it was the one that really made her a performer who wasn't scared to take chances and push the limits of pop music.

# CHAPTER 8: THE 2000s COMEBACK AND GLOBAL DOMINANCE

As the 21st century began, Kylie Minogue was ready for an incredible return after spending a large portion of the 1990s redefining herself as an artist and experimenting with new sounds. Due to two consecutive albums that not only put Kylie back at the top of the mainstream music charts but also made her a cultural icon, the early 2000s saw her achieve worldwide supremacy. Her music struck a chord with a large global audience, and her image came to represent elegance and dance-pop. Her successful comeback to the mainstream was marked with the release of Light Years in 2000, which marked a significant shift from the experimental style of her earlier work, Impossible Princess. This time, Kylie adopted the lively pop sound with disco influences that had always been the foundation of her songs, but she did so with more self-assurance and maturity. It was a celebration of her capacity to change while also embracing pop music's lively, enjoyable elements. Her following release, Fever, which would later become a career milestone, was made possible by Light Years' enormous commercial and critical success. With the September 25, 2000, release of her seventh studio album, Light Years, Kylie Minogue's career saw a comeback. Light Years signaled a dramatic change in her strategy following Impossible Princess's comparatively lackluster commercial performance in the late 1990s. She returned to the pop music that had made her famous with this album, but it had a more nuanced and developed twist.

Dance-pop and disco were the foundations of Light Years' sound, which was greatly influenced by the music of the 1970s and 1980s. Kylie required this fusion of contemporary production methods and vintage inspirations to re-establish herself in the rapidly changing pop music industry. Released on June 19, 2000, "Spinning Around," the album's lead single, swiftly rose to prominence as one of Kylie's most recognizable songs. Before being given to Kylie, the song—which was written by a group that includes pop sensation Paula Abdul—was meant for Abdul's album. Fans were immediately moved by its addictive tune and snappy, lively lyrics. Kylie's "Spinning Around" became her first UK chart-topper in a decade, following "Tears on My Pillow" in 1990. The song immediately shot to the top of the UK Singles Chart. This accomplishment represented Kylie's symbolic return to her status as a pop icon and went beyond a simple commercial triumph. Kylie's reputation as a worldwide celebrity was further solidified with the music video for "Spinning Around." The video, which was directed by Dawn Shadforth, showed Kylie wearing her now-famous gold hotpants, which have come to symbolize her. The video helped reintroduce Kylie to a younger audience by celebrating her self-assured and humorous personality. She became a style icon as a result of those hotpants, which would later become one of the most recognizable fashion items in popular culture. Light Years was a box office success. The album performed well in Australia, where it peaked at number one and debuted at number two on the UK Albums Chart. It also earned double platinum certification in the UK. The catchy duet with Robbie Williams, "Kids," which became another top ten hit, and "On a Night Like This," which also peaked at number two on the UK chart, were among the other big singles it generated. Beyond the financial triumph, Light Years also signaled a shift in the industry's perception of Kylie. She had established herself as a prominent character in dance-pop and had effectively reembraced the pop genre. Light Years' favorable reviews also prepared the ground for Kylie's subsequent album, which would propel her to even higher heights.

# Fever (2001) and the Worldwide Success of "Can't Get You Out of My Head"

On October 1, 2001, Kylie Minogue's eighth studio album, Fever, was released, marking the beginning of her real worldwide dominance. Fever took Kylie's career to a whole new level, building on the success of Light Years. The album immediately became popular, especially in Europe and Australia, where it reached the top of many charts. It became a mainstay of pop music in the early 2000s thanks to its catchy, smooth production and catchy hooks. Kylie's ability to incorporate dance-pop and electronic music components gave the album a new, contemporary feel that appealed to both new listeners and devoted followers. The lead single, "Can't Get You Out of My Head," which was published on September 8, 2001, just a few weeks before the album's release, was unquestionably the highlight of Fever. The song, which was written by Rob Davis and Cathy Dennis, was first offered to Sophie Ellis-Bextor and other performers before Kylie was given it. It turned into the song that defined her career.

Kylie's "Can't Get You Out of My Head" was a unique recording because of its futuristic sound, minimalist production, and mesmerizing "la la la" hook. It was sleek, seductive, and distinctly cool, making it ideal for early 2000s dance floors. The song had an instantaneous and worldwide effect. Along with the UK, Australia, and most of Europe, "Can't Get You Out of My Head" topped the charts in more than 40 nations. The song was Kylie's first major hit in the US since "The Locomotion" in 1988, and it peaked at number seven on the Billboard Hot 100, where she had struggled to find substantial commercial success since her debut. The song became one of the best-selling songs of all time and sold over five million copies worldwide. Kylie's reputation as a pop icon was further cemented by the Dawn Shadforth-directed music video for "Can't Get You Out of My Head." Together with Kylie's recognizable white hooded jumpsuit, the futuristic, avant-garde imagery came to represent the song's slick, contemporary style. The song's popularity grew as a result of the video's extensive rotation on music stations worldwide. The popularity of "Can't Get You Out of My Head" was just the start. Singles like "In Your Eyes," "Love at First Sight," and "Come Into My World" all saw notable commercial success as Fever continued to create hit after hit. While "Come Into My World" won Kylie her first Grammy Award for Best Dance Recording in 2004, In the UK, Australia, and several other nations, "Love at First Sight" went on to become a top-ten hit song. Fever was a commercial and critical success. A uncommon accomplishment for a non-American pop singer at the time, the album went on to earn platinum certification in the US after debuting at number one in Australia and the

UK. It is still regarded as one of the seminal albums of the early 2000s because of its unique fusion of dance-pop, electronic music, and catchy melodies.

## Awards and Recognition in the Early 2000s

The industry acknowledged Kylie Minogue's extraordinary success in the early 2000s with a plethora of honors and recognitions. A period of notable acclaim for Kylie's contributions to mainstream music as well as her ongoing influence as a performer and fashion icon began with the release of Light Years and Fever. Kylie's triumph in the Brit Awards' coveted Best Female Solo Artist category in 2001 demonstrated her renewed supremacy in the UK music industry. After years of being viewed more as a nostalgic figure from the 1980s, Kylie's resurgence as one of the most significant personalities in British pop music made this a significant milestone for her. Kylie's triumph with Fever was further solidified the following year, in 2002, when she was bestowed with numerous accolades. At the 2002 Brit

Awards, she took home two awards: Best International Female Solo Artist and Best International Album for Fever. These victories were especially noteworthy because they demonstrated Fever's widespread popularity and her attractiveness on a worldwide scale. Her breakthrough in Europe was further highlighted that year when she was awarded the NRJ Music Award for Best International Female Artist. When Kylie won her first Grammy Award for Best Dance Recording for "Come Into My World" in 2004, her commercial success and critical praise reached new heights. Kylie's acceptance by the American music industry was marked by this Recording Academy accolade, which was a noteworthy accomplishment.

Her Grammy victory confirmed her reputation as a worldwide celebrity and demonstrated the music's continuing appeal. Apart from these accolades from the business, Kylie's impact went beyond just music. She rose to fame in the fashion industry, inspiring both designers and many admirers with her daring and glitzy look. Her sleek, futuristic appearance from the "Can't Get You Out of My Head" video cemented her as a trendsetter, while her gold hotpants from the "Spinning Around" video became a global sensation. Among many other honors, she received a Woman of the Year award from Glamour magazine in 2007 for her contributions to the fashion industry. In addition to regaining her place at the top of the pop music industry, Kylie Minogue accomplished something even more noteworthy by the early 2000s: she became a worldwide celebrity. Her success with Light Years and Fever demonstrated that she could easily change with the times, and a major contributor to her enduring appeal was her capacity to adopt new styles while retaining her own flair. In addition to being Kylie Minogue's financial zenith, the early 2000s saw her experience tremendous artistic development and widespread acclaim, solidifying her status as one of the greatest pop stars in history.

# CHAPTER 9: BATTLING ADVERSITY: OVERCOMING BREAST CANCER

Kylie Minogue received a breast cancer diagnosis in early May 2005, a few days before she was scheduled to start the Australian leg of her Showgirl: The Greatest Hits tour. She, her fans, and the international entertainment world were all taken aback by the prognosis. The Showgirl tour was intended to be a celebration of Kylie's remarkable career, which had reached its zenith after the enormous success of her albums Light Years and Fever. When Kylie's management made the diagnosis public on May 17, 2005, they disclosed that she had been forced to postpone the remaining dates of her Showgirl tour, which included a much-anticipated appearance at the UK's Glastonbury Festival. Her health was widely publicized by the media, and her fans were devastated worldwide. Since Kylie was not only a well-liked pop artist but also a representation of beauty, strength, and optimism, many people found resonance in her sickness.

After receiving her diagnosis, Kylie started therapy right away, and a few days after the public announcement, she had surgery. She spent a large portion of her recuperation with her family in Melbourne, Australia, where she received treatment.

Due to the nature of her condition, Kylie was forced to permanently halt her profession. As an artist who had always been active and involved in her profession, it was a challenging period for her. Although removing herself from the spotlight was not an easy choice, it was essential for her health and welfare. During her treatment and recuperation, Kylie's absence from the public eye was greatly missed. The cancellation of the Showgirl tour, which had been a huge production, created a gap in the pop music scene. Despite this, Kylie maintained her optimism and hope throughout her fight with cancer, and she often thanked her fans and loved ones for their overwhelming support. Millions of people, especially women battling breast cancer, would find inspiration in her bravery and strength at this time.

# Recovery, the Showgirl Homecoming Tour, and Her Return to Music

Kylie Minogue went into the recuperation stage following months of chemotherapy and surgery. She had finished her first rounds of treatment by the end of 2005 and was gradually regaining her strength. She made sporadic public appearances while still recovering, demonstrating her resolve to get back to her regular routine. After receiving her diagnosis, Kylie made her first appearance on television in November 2005. She thanked her followers for their steadfast support and shared a peek of the personal toll that cancer has placed on her during an emotional interview with Sky News. Her courage and candor about her situation struck a strong chord with the public, and her remarks held great significance for individuals facing comparable challenges. But Kylie's comeback to music took some time. Knowing that her health came first, she took her time getting well. She maintained her connections with her fans and the music industry, however, even during this time. Kylie received the Brit Award for Best

International Female Solo Artist at the beginning of 2006. Her health prevented her from attending the ceremony, but it served as a reminder that her contributions to pop culture and music were nonetheless honored. Kylie finally returned to the stage in November 2006 with the Showgirl: Homecoming tour. Her Showgirl tour, which had been unexpectedly suspended owing to her cancer diagnosis, was being revived with this tour. As the name implies, the Homecoming tour was more than simply a run of shows; it was a symbolic comeback for Kylie and an example of her fortitude and resiliency in the face of hardship. On November 11, 2006, the Showgirl: Homecoming tour began in Sydney, Australia. Fans were excitedly anticipating Kylie's comeback to the stage, and the atmosphere was fantastic. With lavish costumes, exquisite choreography, and a set list full of Kylie's greatest hits, the tour was a stunning celebration of her career. For Kylie and her followers, who had followed her through her illness and recovery, the opening night was a moving occasion. Kylie gave an outstanding performance and showed no indications of slowing down, even though she was still experiencing the physical side effects of her medication. Her energy, theatrical presence, and singing prowess were all as strong as ever.

As Kylie thanked her fans for their love and support during her sickness, the tour was an emotional experience that brought many to tears. The tremendous success of the Showgirl: Homecoming tour solidified Kylie's status as one of the most adored performers in the world. Kylie's return to the music business in the next few years was characterized by her unwavering love of writing and performing. On November 21, 2007, she released X, her ninth studio album and her first following her illness and recuperation. The album, which featured dance-pop songs that embraced life, happiness, and resiliency, was a mirror of her path. X received positive reviews from critics and did well on the charts, peaking at number four in the UK and was nominated for a Grammy for Best Electronic/Dance Album. It was incredible that Kylie was able to make such a strong comeback to the music industry following a life-altering illness. Regaining her position in the industry was only one aspect of her return; she also used it to embrace life after cancer, use her platform to spread awareness, and keep inspiring others with her fortitude and tenacity.

## Public and Personal Support During Her Health Challenges

The public and Kylie Minogue's loved ones showed her unwavering support during her fight with breast cancer. When her diagnosis was revealed in May 2005, fans, singers, and public personalities all sent heartfelt notes. Although Kylie's sickness received a lot of media attention, the tone was one of sympathy and respect for her bravery in enduring such a trying fight. During her diagnosis and treatment, Kylie's family—particularly her parents and siblings—were a vital source of support. She was with her loved ones in Melbourne, Australia, for a large portion of her recuperation. Throughout her treatment, Kylie's mother, Carol Minogue, was there for her both physically and emotionally while she had chemotherapy and surgery. Additionally supporting Kylie was her sister, Dannii Minogue, who frequently provided fans with updates on her health and thanked them for their encouraging words. The French actor Olivier Martinez, Kylie's longtime boyfriend at the time, was a major source of solace in addition to her family. Martinez remained by her side during her medical care, and the media frequently emphasized the couple's bond as an illustration of steadfast support during trying circumstances.

Olivier's presence during this time in Kylie's life was evidence of their strong bond at the time, even though they eventually parted ways. Notable was the outpouring of solidarity from all over the world. Kylie received letters, presents, and encouraging words from fans all over the world. Many of them described their personal experiences fighting cancer or helping loved ones through similar struggles. Later, Kylie said that she was able to get through some of her darkest times thanks to the love and support she received from her followers. Her relationship with her fans only became stronger during this time, and she frequently expressed how lucky she felt to have such a devoted and supportive following. In addition to providing emotional support, Kylie's diagnosis raised public awareness of breast cancer. In a way that few others could, her choice to make her condition public raised awareness of it. The number of young women getting checked for breast cancer significantly increased after her diagnosis, a phenomenon known as the "Kylie effect." Many medical experts believe that Kylie's candor has saved lives by promoting early detection and raising awareness of the value of routine testing. As a well-known person battling illness, Kylie also became an advocate for breast cancer awareness and research. Following her recuperation, she was involved in a number of humanitarian endeavors that supported cancer patients and raised money for cancer research. She frequently discussed how her experience had altered her outlook on life and health, and her work in this field was quite personal. Kylie's reputation as a worldwide figure in fortitude and strength, as well as music, was cemented by her candor and honesty about her health issues and her will to go back on stage and pursue her profession. By confronting her cancer head-on and sharing her story with the world, Kylie Minogue inspired millions of people and demonstrated that one can flourish and shine despite hardship. Her experience with illness and recuperation is evidence of her resilience, character, and lasting influence on the music business, as well as the innumerable lives she has impacted. A striking reminder of life's frailty and the value of perseverance in the face of adversity is provided by Kylie's story of overcoming breast cancer. One of the most important parts of her legacy is still her ability to handle her sickness with dignity while simultaneously using her position to inspire others and spread awareness. Through it all, Kylie Minogue became more than just a musical sensation; she became a global symbol of tenacity and hope.

# CHAPTER 10: FASHION AND STYLE ICON

The impact of Kylie Minogue goes much beyond the realm of music. She has made a name for herself as a global fashion icon throughout her career, influencing trends and working with leading designers across the globe. Her distinctive ability to combine fashion and music in a seamless way has become a crucial aspect of her public identity. Kylie developed close ties with some of the most significant designers in the world early in her career. Her growth as a style icon was largely influenced by these partnerships. Numerous fashion firms, including Jean Paul Gaultier, Dolce & Gabbana, and Julien Macdonald, collaborated closely with her to design ensembles that enhanced her daring stage presence and complimented her musical persona. Her dress choices became more adventurous in the 1990s as she moved away from her previous bubblegum pop persona. Her metamorphosis was greatly aided by Jean-Paul Gaultier, who gave her intricate, cutting-edge creations that defied expectations. Gaultier had previously collaborated with Madonna on the Blonde Ambition tour, and his work with Kylie featured metallic fabrics and striking forms, which helped shape her public persona. Dolce & Gabbana was another important partner in her fashion career. Beginning in the early 2000s, the Italian design team dressed Kylie, creating some of her most iconic ensembles for her 2011 Aphrodite tour and 2001 Fever tour. Their designs frequently blended elegance and sensuality, enabling her to showcase both her smart, mature self and her playful, joyful side.

Kylie's love of these daring and glitzy ensembles contributed to her reputation as a contemporary fashion icon, setting trends all over the world. Kylie's tight partnership with British designer Julien Macdonald further highlighted her capacity to impact fashion. Macdonald, who is renowned for his eye-catching, intricate gown designs, gave Kylie some of her most memorable red carpet experiences. His multi-year collaboration with Kylie helped to establish her as a celebrity who could skillfully combine performance art and high fashion. It is impossible to overestimate the influence of these partnerships on a global scale. Kylie's support of these designers and their designs contributed to the globalization of their work. The golden, sexy pants she wore in the music video for "Spinning Around" in 2000 are among the most well-known instances of this. The hot pants, which were first purchased for just 50 pence at a second-hand retailer, quickly gained popularity. This appearance, which she wore during the promotion for her Light Years record, was a watershed in her career and represented her comeback and self-assurance. In addition to inspiring a variety of fashion imitations, the style thrust those sexy pants into the annals of pop culture. Kylie's impact on fashion was officially acknowledged in 2008 when she was given the prestigious Elle Style Icon Award, which acknowledged her contribution to the development of international fashion. It emphasized how her decisions inspired both followers and fashionistas while also keeping her current in the industry.

# Memorable Red Carpet Moments and Status as a Style Icon

Kylie has continuously taken use of red carpet appearances to highlight her developing sense of style throughout her career. She has made it a priority to make an impression with her wardrobe selections, whether she is attending film premieres, charity galas, or music award events. She won the Best International Female Solo Artist prize at the 2002 Brit Awards, one of her most well-known red carpet moments. She wore a gorgeous Julien Macdonald white satin dress that received accolades from critics for its elegant style and timeless Hollywood appeal. With its exquisite flowing and plunging neckline, the dress showed Kylie's ability to embrace glitzy fashion while maintaining its relevance and modernity. The 2003 Grammy Awards were another memorable occasion. One of the most talked-about looks of the evening was Kylie's stunning gold gown, which was created by Donna Versace. The gown's boldness demonstrated Kylie's confidence as a performer and public personality, while its shimmering fabric and figure-hugging design highlighted her beauty and star power. Over the years, Kylie's style kept changing, but she always managed to leave an impression. She chose to wear a sleek black gown by Stella McCartney, which featured a thigh-high slit and a dramatic one-shoulder design, to the 2014 British Fashion Awards.

Her ability to transition to minimalist fashion while retaining her distinctive glitz was demonstrated by this choice. No matter how trends changed, she was able to maintain her position as a major figure in fashion by finding the ideal balance between sophistication and modernity. Kylie's reputation as a style icon was further cemented by her success on the red carpet. She was welcomed by the fashion industry for her impact on popular culture as well as her daring and sophisticated choices. Because they knew she could pull off ideas that many other celebrities might be afraid to try, fashion experts often commended her for her willingness to take chances. She was a significant muse for many in the fashion industry because her attendance at prominent events often raised awareness of the brands she wore.

# The Evolution of Kylie Minogue's Signature Look

Kylie has developed a distinctive personal style throughout the years, which has changed along with her career. Her early years as a pop sensation were characterized by a vibrant color scheme, striking designs, and whimsical accessories that mirrored the carefree energy of her songs. Her style choices also changed over time, moving from casual to sophisticated as her sound developed. She started experimenting with elegant, minimalist outfits that highlighted her inherent beauty by the late 1990s. Her collaboration with Jean Paul Gaultier was crucial during this time since his futuristic stage costumes symbolized her creative comeback. These designs demonstrated Kylie's newly discovered artistic bravery and were distinguished by metallic fabrics, form-fitting shapes, and bold cuts. Both her music and her reputation underwent a sea change in 2001 with the release of Fever. Her signature style is based on the futuristic, sensual vibe she adopted at this time. One of her most iconic ensembles, the white jumpsuit she wore in the music video for "Can't Get You Out of My Head," represented the stylish, avant-garde persona she had established. Her public reputation as a confident, mature artist was further reconstructed during her Fever tour by her use of edgy, body-conscious apparel.

Kylie's style became a crucial component of her public persona as she carried on creating her legacy. Her elaborate stage clothes contributed to the larger-than-life presence that her fans grew to admire, and they were an integral part of her performances just as much as her songs. Her stage attire always created a statement, whether she was wearing an ornate gown or a showgirl headpiece. Kylie reverted to a more classic, elegant style in the 2010s, choosing classic ensembles that combined glitz with a contemporary twist. Her public appearances tended more toward elegant, form-fitting clothes and high-end couture, even though her daring theatrical attire continued to be a significant aspect of her performing character. Her ability to stay up to date while maintaining her sense of style was further highlighted by her partnerships with companies like Stella McCartney.

The most recognizable item in her wardrobe is still the golden hot pants from "Spinning Around," which not only mark a significant turning point in her career but also demonstrate her ability to transform an ordinary article of apparel into a cultural icon. Kylie's continued importance in the music and fashion sectors may be attributed in large part to her willingness to make daring decisions both on and off stage. Kylie Minogue's ability to stay ahead of trends while staying true to her artistic vision is demonstrated by her fashion journey. She has made a lasting impression on the fashion industry with her partnerships with leading designers, her memorable red carpet appearances, and the creation of her own style. Her status as a true fashion innovator and pop star is cemented as her style impact continues to speak to new generations of followers.

# CHAPTER 11: PERSONAL LIFE AND RELATIONSHIPS

Known as a pop icon and cultural personality, Kylie Minogue has been in the spotlight for a large portion of her life. Behind the music, the flashing cameras, and the hectic pace of her international career, however, is a very personal story that is full of important relationships, personal turning points, and the ongoing struggle to strike a balance between her desire for a normal existence and her celebrity. Kylie has shown an amazing capacity to maintain her personal boundaries while navigating the heavy public scrutiny that comes with being a celebrity, from her first relationships to her times of personal triumph and vulnerability. Since Kylie's sexual relationships are frequently featured in tabloid headlines, her love life has long been a source of fascination. Beginning in 1989, she had her first significant public relationship with INXS's mysterious lead singer, Michael Hutchence. Due to their disparate public perceptions, Hutchence and Kylie were one of the most well-known couples of the late 1980s and early 1990s. Their partnership captivated the media. At the time, Hutchence was the quintessential rock star renegade, while Kylie was just off her "girl next door" success as Charlene on Neighbours and was becoming a global pop phenomenon. As Kylie herself acknowledged in subsequent interviews, the relationship was powerful and passionate, but it also introduced her to a side of life that was very different from her previously insulated way of living.

Before splitting up, their relationship lasted for almost two years, yet it had a lasting impact on Kylie's public image. Kylie acknowledged that Hutchence had introduced her to the wilder, more liberated sides of life when she looked back on their time together, even years after his untimely death in 1997. Following Hutchence, Kylie had a number of well-publicized relationships, all of which were heavily covered by the media. Her 2003 romance with French actor Olivier Martinez was one of her longest-lasting partnerships. The pair frequently appeared in photos together when traveling to Paris and London and attending red carpet events. Even though the public found their connection fascinating, Kylie and Olivier were able to keep most of their personal lives out of the newspapers, only making sporadic remarks about their relationship. Throughout Kylie's fight with breast cancer in 2005, Martinez was especially encouraging and supported her throughout the most trying time in her life. He provided both emotional and physical assistance throughout that period, which she has frequently acknowledged as a major source of strength. However, their partnership ended peacefully in 2007, with both parties pointing to the stress of sustaining a committed relationship in the spotlight as a contributing reason. In 2008, Kylie started dating model Andrés Velencoso, with whom she had another important relationship. The five-year relationship between Kylie and Spanish model Velencoso was frequently characterized as one of her most secure and personal. Even when rumors about marriage and having kids circulated, the couple was able to keep a large portion of their relationship out of the public eye by hardly discussing their personal lives. The artist Kylie has addressed these personal decisions in interviews, and her decision to not get married and have kids has frequently been the subject of media attention. She has publicly acknowledged that although she had previously envisioned a conventional family life for herself, the pressures of her job and her personal situation caused her to choose a different course. Once further demonstrating the challenge of sustaining love relationships when under continual public scrutiny, her relationship with Velencoso terminated in 2013. In 2015, Kylie got into another well-known relationship, this time with Joshua Sasse, a British actor.

Early in 2016, the couple got engaged after their romance quickly bloomed while filming the television series Galavant. Kylie appeared to have found long-term bliss for a while, as Sasse even openly expressed his admiration for her. However, due to allegations of Sasse's infidelity, their relationship terminated in 2017. Later, Kylie discussed the emotional toll of the split, acknowledging that she was devastated by the engagement's termination. Even though their relationship was widely known, Kylie once again handled the breakup with poise, deciding to put more of an emphasis on her music and recuperation than on stoking the tabloid rumors. Kylie has always taken a measuredly open approach to relationships. She has never hesitated to acknowledge her love partners, but she has also been quite careful of her personal life because she knows that being famous frequently comes at the expense of one's privacy. Kylie has consistently struck a careful balance over the years between giving the public access to her private life and shielding the most private parts of it from prying eyes. In a field that frequently feeds on scandal and oversharing, her ability to handle the complications of fame and relationships has allowed her to preserve some degree of personal integrity.

## Personal Milestones and Navigating Life Outside the Spotlight

Numerous significant events in Kylie Minogue's life, both happy and challenging, have molded her into the strong person she is today. When she received a breast cancer diagnosis in 2005 at the age of 36, it was one of the biggest personal setbacks she had ever experienced. Both Kylie and her fans were taken aback by the prognosis, especially because she was then in the middle of her Showgirl tour. Fans all throughout the world showed their support when Kylie revealed in May 2005 that the tour would be canceled in order to concentrate on her treatment.

Shortly after receiving the diagnosis, she had chemotherapy and surgery in Melbourne. Kylie kept as quiet as possible during her fight with cancer, giving the public very few updates. Throughout her treatment, her family—especially her parents and sister Dannii—provided both emotional and physical support, which was important in her rehabilitation. Her then-partner Olivier Martinez also stuck by her side, going to doctor's appointments with her and providing unwavering support. In subsequent interviews, Kylie would describe this time as a time of significant emotional and physical change. Her cancer experience changed her outlook on life, making her value family, health, and time away from the demands of the workplace. Kylie triumphantly returned to the stage in 2006 with the Showgirl Homecoming tour, following her successful completion of treatment. In addition to commemorating her recuperation, the tour demonstrated her continued bond with her followers, many of whom had been there for her during her illness. Kylie's decision to resume singing was a major turning point in her life and confirmed her place as one of pop's most adored icons. However, in spite of her public image, Kylie kept a rather private existence off the stage, preferring to concentrate on her health and wellbeing in the years after her recuperation. Along with her fight with cancer, Kylie has accomplished a lot in her personal life, much of which she has shared with her devoted fan base. Her 50th birthday was commemorated in 2018, marking an important turning point in both her personal and professional lives. Her journey through love, heartbreak, and self-discovery was portrayed on the album Golden, which she released to commemorate the event. The album, which featured country undertones, was a change from Kylie's typical pop sound and revealed a more reflective side of herself. It served as a reminder that even after decades of being in the spotlight, Kylie remained a very private artist who was not afraid to express her deepest feelings and ideas via her music.

Kylie's longevity has always been largely attributed to her ability to handle life away from the spotlight. Even though she is unquestionably one of the most well-known women in the world, she has managed to keep her sense of self and rejuvenate by carving apart a private existence. Kylie has frequently discussed the significance of balance in interviews, admitting that although she enjoys her job, she also cherishes time spent with friends and family away from the demands of celebrity. Kylie has always put her health first, making sure she gets the time and space to think and develop as a person, whether she is spending time with her family in Australia or retreating to her home in London.

## The Media's Interest in Her Personal Life

Kylie Minogue has been a media sensation since the start of her career. She shot to popularity on the Australian serial show Neighbours in the 1980s, and her subsequent climb to international music stardom only heightened media interest in her private life. Every facet of Kylie's life, from her love relationships to her fashion choices, has been extensively covered by the media throughout the years, frequently treating her private life events as public property. She was under a lot of media attention in the late 1980s, especially when she was dating Michael Hutchence. Since Kylie and Hutchence were both at the height of their stardom, the media was always analyzing their relationship and making predictions about how compatible they would be and how their romance would develop.

Kylie was able to keep a respectful quiet in the face of the heightened scrutiny, hardly ever discussing the specifics of their relationship. Throughout her career, Kylie's handling of the media's interest in her personal life would be characterized by this strategy. Kylie continued to come under media attention in the years after her romance with Hutchence, especially when she was seeing Olivier Martinez and Joshua Sasse. False rumors and inflated stories were frequently the result of the media's fixation with Kylie's love life, but Kylie always stayed out of the spotlight and chose to concentrate on her career rather than react to the tabloid headlines. Kylie was able to remain in control of the story even during her breast cancer diagnosis and treatment, releasing health updates when needed but keeping the more intimate details of her experience confidential. Even though Kylie is now in her 50s, the media's interest in her private life has never diminished. Nevertheless, despite all, Kylie has maintained her position as one of the most esteemed personalities in the entertainment sector, valued for her skill as well as her composure and fortitude in the face of unrelenting media attention. One of Kylie Minogue's distinguishing traits is her capacity to ignore the frequently intrusive attention. She has resisted the urge to overshare or publicly defend her private choices, and she has never let the media's fixation on her personal life overwhelm her professional accomplishments. She has instead opted for a discreet approach, letting her music and artistic creations speak for themselves while carefully limiting the aspects of her private life that she makes public. Kylie has talked candidly over the years about the negative effects that life in the spotlight can have on one's mental health and general wellbeing. She has been open in interviews about how difficult it is to lead a private life when the media is watching you all the time. Although she is aware of the attention her public image generates, she has admitted that, in order to maintain her own feeling of normalcy, she keeps some parts of her private life completely private. Kylie's long-term success and her capacity to keep a positive connection with celebrities have been greatly aided by her ability to establish limits. Kylie's choice to remain single and childless has been one of the most recurring themes in the media's portrayal of her private life. The media has frequently conjectured about Kylie's sexual life throughout her career, specifically whether or not she will ever get married and have children.

She has graciously responded to these inquiries by stating that although she initially had a more conventional career in mind, life has taken her in a different direction. She has talked candidly about how she has come to terms with her choices and the emotional difficulties of acknowledging that she might never have children. Her followers, who respect her strength and vulnerability in handling such a delicate subject in the public eye, have only grown to love her more as a result of her candor about such a highly personal subject. Kylie's public image has also been greatly influenced by the media's fascination with her style and fashion. Throughout her career, Kylie has been a style icon, setting the standard for fashion and influencing trends, from her early days as Charlene in Neighbours to her glitzy pop star makeover. Her stage costumes and red carpet appearances have garnered a lot of media attention, and the press has frequently concentrated on her fashion choices. Even in this area of her public life, though, Kylie has maintained control over her image by expressing herself through fashion rather than letting her looks define her. Kylie has adjusted to the changing ways that the public consumes celebrity news in more recent years as the media environment has changed due to the emergence of social media and online gossip. Even though she is still quite visible, she has become even pickier about what she shares with the world, interacting with her admirers on her own terms through social media sites like Instagram. Kylie has maintained a degree of privacy that is becoming more and more uncommon in today's hyperconnected society by controlling her social media presence and only sharing tidbits of her personal life. In many respects, Kylie's connection with the media is evidence of her unwavering professionalism and in-depth knowledge of the entertainment sector. She has always been cautious to keep control of her own tale and has never let the media determine the parameters of her public narrative. In addition to shielding her from the more negative impacts of tabloid culture, her cautious handling of celebrities has helped her maintain her status as a well-liked and esteemed public figure.

# CHAPTER 12: PHILANTHROPY AND PUBLIC INFLUENCE

Kylie Minogue's public impact and charitable endeavors go much beyond her musical career. She has continuously shown a strong dedication to humanitarian work, supporting issues ranging from environmental campaigning to children's health and cancer research. Her reputation as a devoted philanthropist and a cherished cultural icon has been further cemented by the substantial awareness she has been able to create for numerous global causes thanks to her platform, which she has developed over decades in the entertainment business. Raising awareness of breast cancer, a topic that is very close to Kylie's heart, has been one of the most important facets of her charitable endeavors. At the age of 36, Kylie received a breast cancer diagnosis in 2005, a turning point in her life that also changed her impact on the global scene. Her choice to make her diagnosis public raised a remarkable amount of awareness about the significance of cancer research and early detection.

Kylie had already participated in a number of humanitarian endeavors prior to her illness, but this event signaled a change in direction, making her advocacy more urgent and targeted.

Particularly in her native Australia, where there was an estimated 40% rise in breast cancer screenings following her public disclosure of her illness, Kylie's candor about her experience with breast cancer had a significant influence on cancer screening awareness. Some have called her impact on health-related awareness the "Kylie effect," which demonstrates the scope of her platform. She connected with people through her personal health struggle, highlighting the value of early detection, which became a hot topic in public health conversations. In addition to spreading awareness, Kylie has partnered with a number of nonprofits and actively participated in initiatives that assist cancer patient care and research funding. Using her famous position to raise awareness of these causes, she has backed groups including Breast Cancer Care, Cancer Research UK, and the National Breast Cancer Foundation in Australia. Kylie is actively involved in campaigns, charity events, and fundraisers that benefit cancer patients and survivors; her commitment goes beyond endorsements. Beyond her efforts to support causes relating to cancer, Kylie has expanded her charitable interests to include the health and welfare of children. Great Ormond Street Hospital, a well-known children's hospital in London, has been one of her longstanding charity affiliations. She has regularly contributed to the hospital's initiatives and run public awareness campaigns to raise the standard of care for children who are very sick. Kylie's many unpublicized hospital trips demonstrate her sincere concern for the problem rather than her desire for attention. Her strong dedication to philanthropic work is further demonstrated by her personal relationships with these kids, their families, and the medical personnel. Since the 1990s, Kylie has been an outspoken advocate for HIV prevention and AIDS awareness, two causes that are also very important to her. Kylie has taken part in campaigns and fundraising events that have raised millions of dollars for AIDS research as one of the international ambassadors for amfAR, The Foundation for AIDS Research. Given her close ties to the LGBTQ+

community, which has traditionally been impacted by the HIV/AIDS crisis, her dedication to this cause is especially noteworthy. Beyond her famous profile, Kylie has taken on a significant role in the struggle against the stigmatization of HIV and AIDS.

In addition to supporting particular health causes, Kylie has been actively involved in environmental campaigning, supporting international initiatives to save the environment and fight climate change. She has taken part in activities like Live Earth, a global concert series that was organized in 2007 to raise awareness of climate change. Through her participation, Kylie has urged her global fan base to embrace environmentally friendly behaviors and provide their support to conservation initiatives. Even though media attention may not always focus on Kylie's environmental advocacy, she has continuously demonstrated her commitment to bringing attention to the pressing need to save the world.

# Her Advocacy for Cancer Research and Other Humanitarian Efforts

One of Kylie's most important charitable endeavors continues to be her support of cancer research. Following her diagnosis, she emerged as a strong voice in favor of funding ongoing cancer research as well as early detection. Because of her campaigning, the public's perception of breast cancer has changed, and it is now a subject that is more widely discussed and comprehended. In order to support research groups, Kylie has participated in a number of fundraising events, frequently contributing a portion of her ticket sales or selling personal items at auction. Her advocacy for cancer research has expanded to a global scale. Kylie performed at a benefit performance in the UK in 2008, three years after receiving her initial diagnosis and treatment. All revenues from the event were donated to cancer research. She has also contributed to campaigns in Australia and the UK by making appearances in PSAs that stress the value of medical research and promote routine cancer screenings. Kylie's public persona has played a significant role in dispelling the stigma associated with breast cancer, especially among younger women who may have previously thought they were not in danger. Kylie's activism goes beyond awareness-raising and fundraising. She has used her platform to highlight the significance of mental health care for individuals battling cancer and to speak openly about the emotional toll that the disease can take on patients and their families. Because of her own experience, she is able to provide a degree of understanding and empathy that appeals to people going through comparable difficulties. Kylie is a well-liked person in the cancer survivor community because of her willingness to be vulnerable, and she still supports research and helps people who are impacted by the disease.

In addition to her engagement with cancer-related causes, Kylie has continuously backed humanitarian aid and disaster relief initiatives. Kylie was quick to give her help following the 2004 Indian Ocean tsunami, which was one of the deadliest natural disasters in modern history. She gave a sizable amount of her earnings to relief efforts and took part in performances to raise money. Over 230,000 people were killed and millions were displaced by the tsunami, and the international response from artists like Kylie helped raise much-needed money to help reconstruct towns. She has also supported underprivileged communities as part of her humanitarian efforts. Kylie has long supported equality and rights for LGBTQ+ people. Given that she has embraced her role as a homosexual icon throughout her career, this facet of her generosity has been especially significant. As part of her LGBTQ+ advocacy, Kylie has supported marriage equality campaigns, taken part in Pride events, and collaborated with groups like The Trevor Project, which aims to prevent suicide among LGBTQ+ adolescents. Within the LGBTQ+ community, she is widely respected and admired for her dedication to the community. At the British LGBT Awards in 2019, Kylie received the Ally Award in recognition of her continued advocacy for LGBTQ+ issues and her status as a beloved community ally. She has consistently advocated for inclusivity over the years, encouraging her fans and followers to value diversity and against discrimination.

## Public Influence and the Power of Her Platform

The public impact of Kylie Minogue goes well beyond her musical career. She has become a powerful voice in philanthropy, fashion, health awareness, and social issues thanks to her ability to use her platform. Because of her devoted following and her reputation as a worldwide celebrity, she has been able to raise awareness of important topics that could otherwise go unnoticed. The sincere bond Kylie has with her fans is one of the distinctive features of her public influence. Kylie's charity endeavors are quite personal, and she handles them with honesty and attention, in contrast to many celebrities whose charitable work may come out as aloof or detached. Because of her genuineness, she has been able to encourage millions of others to support the causes she believes in. In addition to generating millions of dollars in donations, her charitable endeavors have spurred discussions on significant topics, especially those pertaining to LGBTQ+ rights and cancer research. Numerous groups have acknowledged Kylie's dedication to using her platform for good, and she has won countless accolades for her efforts. Because of her contributions to philanthropy and music, she was named an Officer of the Order of the British Empire (OBE) in 2008. This distinction highlighted the influence she has had on society by acknowledging her contributions to the arts as well as her broad charity activity. Kylie Minogue has used her public platform to bring about long-lasting change through her activism, humanitarian endeavors, and philanthropic activities. She is one of the most admired and respected persons in the entertainment industry because of her capacity to relate to people on a personal level and her unrelenting commitment to issues that are important to her. As she advances in her profession, her charitable legacy will continue to be a significant aspect of her public life, and her platform remains a potent force for good.

# CHAPTER 13: MUSICAL LONGEVITY AND INNOVATION

Kylie Minogue's ability to adapt and stay relevant in the rapidly changing music industry has been a defining feature of her career. She demonstrated a remarkable talent for reinvention, creative experimentation, and sustained success on the international scene throughout the 2010s and into the 2020s. Her versatility is demonstrated by her albums Aphrodite (2010), Golden (2018), and Disco (2020), which show a path that not only welcomes innovation but also solidifies her status as a timeless pop star. Kylie had established herself as a master of reinvention by the time she released Aphrodite in 2010. But this album signaled yet another important change. Kylie started a journey that would see her return to the more exuberant, euphoric side of pop music after the success of her earlier albums, especially Fever (2001) and X (2007), which solidified her position as a dance-pop queen. Aphrodite was a celebration of her legacy and her innovative pop style. "All the Lovers," the album's debut song, was widely praised when it was released in June 2010. With its soaring melody and emotionally charged lyrics, it turned into a hymn of unity and celebration. The single was a commercial success, peaking at number three in the UK and making it to the top 10 in many other countries. The popularity of the song established the tone for the remainder of the album, which was strongly impacted by themes of joy, empowerment, and love. Aphrodite, which was produced by Stuart Price, was a polished, well-organized collection of work that demonstrated Kylie's self-assurance in her artistic identity.

Price, who is well-known for working with artists like Madonna and The Killers, contributed to the album's development into a vibrant, dancefloor-friendly compilation that was distinctively Kylie while also demonstrating her sound's development and maturity. Kylie became the first solo artist to have a number one album in four successive decades (the 1980s, 1990s, 2000s, and 2010s) when the album itself debuted at the top of the UK Albums Chart. This accomplishment alone demonstrated her unmatched capacity to be relevant for many generations. Songs like "Get Outta My Way" and "Better Than Today" further highlighted her commitment to the dance-pop genre, with captivating beats and uplifting lyrics that resonated with both long-time fans and new listeners. The success of Aphrodite was a testament to Kylie's unique ability to mix nostalgia with modernity, making an album that paid homage to her past while simultaneously pushing her sound ahead.

However, the true surprise came in 2018 with the release of Golden, an album that saw Kylie pushing her music in an altogether new direction. Moving away from the electronic pop and dance music that had defined much of her career, Golden was laced with country and folk influences, indicating a striking change from her prior work. The shift was partly inspired by her time spent recording in Nashville, Tennessee, a city known for its long traditions in country music. The experience of working in such a diverse musical setting helped Kylie dig into new emotional depths and songwriting methods. The mood of the album was established right away by the lead single, "Dancing," which was released in January 2018. With its infectious pop tune and country twang, the song demonstrated Kylie's willingness to try out different genres without sacrificing her distinctively cheerful voice. Because the lyrics focused on living life to the fullest despite hardship, the song also served as a mirror of her own tenacity. Her lyrics, "When I go out, I wanna go out dancing," struck a chord with admirers who had followed her through the highs and lows of her career and personal life. Golden, which debuted at the top of the UK Albums Chart, was a commercial and critical success. The album's distinctive pop and country fusion and its intensely personal lyrics demonstrated Kylie's courage to take chances and go against the grain. Songs like "A Lifetime to Repair" and "Stop Me from Falling" further demonstrated her ability to meld genres in a way that felt both original and genuine. In addition, Kylie used this time to reflect on herself, as evidenced by the album's themes of love, heartbreak, and self-discovery. Kylie poured her feelings into her music after her engagement to actor Joshua Sasse ended in 2017, creating an album that was more personal and reflective than most of her earlier work. Songs like "Sincerely Yours" and "Music's Too Sad Without You" (a duet with British singer Jack Savoretti) had a lot of emotional impact, which helped fans better understand Kylie's personal journey during this period.

## The Release of Disco (2020) and Continuing to Dominate the Pop Charts

Disco, Kylie's 2020 album, was released as the globe was still dealing with the COVID-19 pandemic's repercussions. Kylie once again demonstrated her ability to adjust and succeed in any situation, even in the face of the difficulties plaguing the music industry. With a new, modern twist, disco was a return to the dance-pop foundations that had made her a worldwide star. The glitzy, glamorous world of disco from the 1970s served as the inspiration for the record. This music is renowned for its contagious energy and positive sentiments, which were much needed in the uncertain year of 2020. Disco, which was released in November 2020, was a critical and financial success. When the lead song, "Say Something," was released in July 2020, it received accolades for both its glittering production and its positive message. Listeners who were negotiating the loneliness and uncertainty of the pandemic found resonance in the song's lyrics, which read, "Love is love; it never ends; can we all be as one again?" The song was praised for its ability to convey the escapist and emotional aspects of disco music, and it soon became a fan favorite.

Disco's popularity went well beyond only its hit song. Kylie became the first woman to have a number-one album in five decades when the album debuted at the top of the UK Albums Chart. This amazing accomplishment demonstrated her resilience in the music business and her capacity to continuously create music that appeals to both critics and fans. Songs like "Magic" and "I Love It" were among the album's other highlights, demonstrating Kylie's talent for writing catchy, upbeat pop hits. The production, which was strongly influenced by disco music from the 1970s, was a wonderful fit for Kylie's lively, vivacious personality. Disco was a celebration of Kylie's musical heritage as well as her ongoing ability to push the boundaries of pop music. Kylie's active involvement in the creation of Disco was one of its most noteworthy features. The pandemic forced Kylie to record a large portion of the album in her home studio, where she also served as producer and engineer for the first time in her career. She was able to mold the album's direction and tone in a way that felt really intimate and true to her artistic vision, thanks to this increased creative freedom. Disco's release also signaled the start of a new phase in Kylie's live performing career. Since the pandemic prevented traditional touring, Kylie made accommodations by developing Infinite Disco, a virtual concert experience that was streamed worldwide in November 2020. Featuring beautiful costumes, choreography, and special effects, the performance was a visually stunning, high-energy event that captured the essence of the disco era. Infinite Disco's success further proved Kylie's capacity for creativity and audience engagement despite previously unheard-of difficulties.

# Discovering New Creative Paths in Entertainment and Music

Kylie's readiness to follow new creative paths has been a major factor in her success and relevance over the past thirty years. From her earliest days as a soap opera star to her current position as the "Princess of Pop," Kylie has never been satisfied with her success and has continuously pushed the limits of her craft. Beyond music, Kylie has pursued other artistic endeavors in recent years. She has dabbled in acting, fashion, and even winemaking, each of which has demonstrated her adaptability and spirit of entrepreneurship. She started her own wine company, Kylie Minogue Wines, in 2020, and it soon achieved success in the marketplace. A variety of rosé, white, and sparkling wines are offered under the brand, which embodies Kylie's attention to detail and dedication to excellence. Her reputation as a versatile entertainer and businesswoman has been further cemented by the endeavor. Kylie's ability to adjust to shifting trends while maintaining her distinct artistic personality is evidence of her ongoing success in the music business. Whether channeling the disco vibes on Disco or dabbling with country influences on Golden, Kylie has never shied away from taking chances and pushing her creative boundaries. She continues to be a powerful force in the pop industry because of her openness to embracing new ideas and sounds, which has kept her music interesting and fresh.

Along with her business endeavors and musical endeavors, Kylie has persisted in looking into acting roles. Despite concentrating mostly on her singing career in recent years, she has made a number of noteworthy TV and movie appearances, notably costarring with Dwayne "The Rock" Johnson in the 2015 movie San Andreas. She reminded viewers of her flexibility as an entertainer by showcasing her acting skills in the catastrophe movie as Susan Riddick. Looking ahead, Kylie's capacity for innovation and change indicates that she will keep surprising and delighting her admirers for many years to come. She continues to establish herself as one of the most vibrant and resilient personalities in contemporary pop culture with every new endeavor. Her talent for reinvention and originality, whether in music, business, or other creative ventures, has set her apart from many of her peers. Kylie Minogue's lasting relevance is not merely a result of luck or nostalgia; it's a product of her constant quest for new artistic boundaries, her openness to embrace change, and her ability to anticipate and adapt to evolving societal trends.

# CHAPTER 14: CULTURAL IMPACT AND GAY ICON STATUS

The cultural significance of Kylie Minogue goes well beyond her mainstream music accomplishments. In the LGBTQ+ community, she has gained immense significance as a result of her music, persona, and tenacity, which have solidified her reputation as a homosexual icon. Throughout her career, Kylie has developed a devoted and multigenerational fan following that is bound together by a love of her music, style, and presence. She has become a permanent fixture in the global musical landscape due to her cultural influence on LGBTQ+ audiences and her impact on the direction of pop music. When Kylie Minogue first gained international recognition in the late 1980s with songs like "I Should Be So Lucky" (1987) and "Better the Devil You Know" (1990), her relationship with the LGBTQ+ community began. Gay men were especially moved by these songs' catchy melodies and lively production, and many of them found joy and freedom in

Kylie's music at a time when the AIDS epidemic was wreaking havoc on their community. Her early work's energy and optimism served as a means of celebration and escape, and her stage appearance only served to win over LGBTQ+ followers. Kylie's relationship with the LGBTQ+ community had developed into something more profound by the time she released Fever in 2001. "Can't Get You Out of My Head," the album's lead hit, became an anthem for many fans, particularly in the gay community. Kylie's slick, robotic dancing, futuristic production, and catchy chorus all contributed to the hyperstylized, camp look that many LGBTQ+ fans loved. During this time, she also capitalized on the theatricality and sense of spectacle that had long been popular in LGBTQ+ culture through her live performances and music videos, which were marked by lavish costumes and creative staging. Kylie's reputation as a lesbian icon has been greatly influenced by her sense of style and fashion. She has proven throughout her career to have a special ability to strike a balance between high glamour and approachable pop appeal, which has made her a popular choice among LGBTQ+

followers, especially those in the drag and performance communities. As a visual symbol of her fusion of sex appeal and a carefree attitude, her famous gold hot pants, which she wore in the music video for "Spinning Around" (2000), became an indelible part of pop cultural history. LGBTQ+ followers have praised Kylie for her openness to embrace both femininity and camp; many of them regard her as a symbol of the freedom to be oneself without feeling guilty. In addition to her style and music, Kylie's public presence has helped to establish her as a homosexual icon.

She has been outspoken in her support of equality and has continuously demonstrated her unflinching support for LGBTQ+ rights. It has been especially crucial for her to keep up a close personal relationship with her LGBTQ+ fan group. Kylie has frequently expressed her gratitude for her homosexual fans' support, attributing it to their assistance in sustaining her career throughout its various stages. To further establish herself in the community, she has also taken part in a number of LGBTQ+ events, such as performing at Pride celebrations in Sydney, London, and New York. Kylie's fight with breast cancer in 2005 only strengthened her bond with her LGBTQ+ followers. Her fortitude during her treatment and her candor about the difficulties she encountered struck a profound chord with a community that had long struggled for visibility and survival, especially during the AIDS pandemic. As a show of solidarity, Kylie's openness to share her story and her subsequent recovery bolstered her relationship with her LGBTQ+ fan base. The fact that Kylie's music and image are still prevalent in LGBT nightlife is one of the most important indicators of her standing as a gay icon. Around the world, her songs are a mainstay at clubs, drag shows, and Pride celebrations. Kylie's music and style have been frequently praised by drag artists in particular, who frequently incorporate her hallmark songs and looks into their shows. Her impact on the LGBTQ+ performance scene is evidence of how her music has moved beyond its initial setting and integrated into a common cultural experience that honors joy, freedom, and identity.

## Her Influence on Future Pop Stars and Her Enduring Fanbase

It is impossible to overstate Kylie Minogue's impact on upcoming pop star generations. Numerous musicians who have come after her have been influenced by her ability to switch between musical genres with ease while retaining her own style. Kylie has been regarded as an influence by numerous modern pop singers, such as Lady Gaga, Dua Lipa, and Carly Rae Jepsen, especially for her ability to strike a balance between popular appeal and a devoted LGBTQ+ fan base. Specifically, Lady Gaga has discussed Kylie's influence on her own career in public. In interviews, Gaga has commended Kylie for her ability to change without losing her identity, emphasizing how her songs blend catchy pop melodies with more profound emotional depth. Gaga's extravagant stage presence and dramatic performances are reminiscent of the spectacle that Kylie has long loved, especially in her later career. Another pop sensation who has had a lot of success recently, Dua Lipa, has also acknowledged Kylie's impact. The two musicians worked together in 2020 to remix Kylie's song "Real Groove," which was included on the Disco album. The partnership was a time of mutual appreciation, as Kylie praised Dua Lipa's innovative approach to pop music and Dua Lipa expressed her love for Kylie's work. This intergenerational bond emphasizes Kylie's function as a link between the past and present in the music industry. Beyond her impact on individual musicians, one of Kylie's most impressive professional achievements has been her ability to sustain a devoted following across several decades. She has received unwavering support from her LGBTQ+ fan base in particular, which has kept her going throughout her career. Kylie's emotional bond with her fans is what distinguishes her from many other pop stars.

Her music is a source of solace, strength, and happiness rather than only serving as the background music for their lives. This ongoing bond is demonstrated by her live performances. Fans from many walks of life gather to enjoy Kylie's concerts, which are renowned for their inclusion and joyous atmosphere. Kylie has the rare ability to make every fan feel recognized and valued, whether she's playing in a large arena or a smaller setting. In the LGBTQ+ community, where her music has come to represent emancipation and self-expression, this bond is especially deep. Another noteworthy aspect of Kylie's fan base is its variety. Although she is frequently linked to her LGBTQ+ fan base, her appeal cuts across age, gender, and sexual orientation. The universality of her music, which touches on themes of love, resiliency, and joy, is demonstrated by her ability to connect with such a diverse fan base. Kylie is one of the most adored pop performers in the world because of her wide appeal, which has guaranteed that her influence transcends all demographics.

## The Legacy of Her Music in Global Pop Culture

There is no denying Kylie Minogue's influence on popular culture around the world. She has released numerous successes during her career, which have woven themselves into the fabric of popular music. Songs like "Love at First Sight," "Can't Get You Out of

My Head," and "Spinning Around" are not merely catchy pop tunes; they are cultural icons that have shaped whole musical periods. Kylie's longevity in a famously erratic industry is demonstrated by her ability to continuously produce hits that reach the top of the charts across several decades. Both the way her music continues to appeal to new generations of fans and the work of modern musicians are examples of her impact. Younger audiences who might not have been familiar with Kylie's early work have become aware of her music thanks to the growth of streaming services like Spotify and Apple Music. As new listeners realize how timeless her music is, this has helped to guarantee that her legacy keeps expanding. Kylie has had a huge influence on pop culture and fashion in addition to her musical achievements. From the bubblegum pop aesthetic of the late 1980s to the high-end glamor of her latter career, her style has changed with time. In terms of fashion, Kylie has always been at the forefront, and her impact can be seen in the creations of stylists, designers, and avant-garde artists worldwide. The cultural influence Kylie has had on the world is just as significant as her musical contributions. As a pop sensation, a survivor, and an LGBT icon, Kylie Minogue embodies the strength of resiliency, self-expression, and reinvention. For millions of people worldwide, she is a symbol of strength and empowerment because of her music, her style, and her consistent support for the LGBTQ+ community.

# CHAPTER 15: AWARDS, HONORS, AND MILESTONES

Kylie Minogue has had an absolutely remarkable path through the entertainment sector. Her career, which spanned more than thirty years, is marked by a number of noteworthy accolades, distinctions, and achievements that bear witness to her influence as a performer, artist, and cultural icon. Kylie has continuously been acknowledged for her diverse abilities, from earning major international honors like the Grammy, Brit Awards, and ARIA Awards to being honored for her contributions to popular culture, fashion, and philanthropy. She has broken records, accomplished great feats, and left a lasting legacy throughout her career. Her significant accolades, distinctions, and career turning points that have cemented her legacy in music and entertainment are covered in detail in this chapter. With major honors from some of the most prestigious music institutions, Kylie Minogue's accolades demonstrate her enduring skill and global influence. The most noteworthy of these occurred in 2004, when her smash song "Come into My World" earned her the Grammy Award for Best Dance Recording. After multiple nominations, Kylie's first Grammy victory was a turning point in her career. Even though "Come into My World," from her 2001 album Fever, had already solidified her place as a pop legend, Kylie's Grammy victory represented a new degree of global recognition, particularly in the cutthroat U.S. market. Kylie is one of Australia's most renowned musical exports, having won multiple ARIA Awards (Australian Recording Industry Association Awards) in her own country. Over the years, she has remained a strong presence at the ARIAs, winning her first ARIA Award in 1988 for her breakthrough self-titled album, Kylie.

In recognition of her lifelong contributions to the Australian music business, Kylie was inducted into the ARIA Hall of Fame in 2011 and has won awards in categories such as Best Pop Release and Best Female Artist. Her induction into the ARIA Hall of Fame was a moving occasion that honored her heritage while celebrating her global accomplishments. Additionally,

Kylie has received multiple honors at the Brit Awards, one of the UK's most prominent music award shows. Her success with the Fever album was reflected in her first Brit Award, which she received in 2002 for Best International Female Solo Artist. In 2008, during the X period, she was given the same honor once more, confirming her sustained supremacy in the global music industry. Along with these victories, Kylie has received other Brit Award nominations throughout the years, further solidifying her reputation as a significant player in the international music scene. Other noteworthy honors include the World Music Awards, where Kylie won the World's Best-Selling Australian Artist title in 2001 and 2002, and the MTV Europe Music Awards, where she has received numerous accolades. These accolades demonstrate her wide commercial appeal and ongoing global fame. These honors, which span continents and audiences, demonstrate the music's enormous global appeal.

# Special Recognitions in Music, Fashion, and Philanthropy

In addition to the numerous accolades Kylie has gotten for her music, she has also received recognition in a number of other areas, most notably fashion and philanthropy, where she has made important contributions. Kylie's influence on fashion has always been a significant aspect of her artistic identity, and she has received numerous accolades for her sense of style throughout the years. She received the coveted Elle Style Award for Woman of the Year in 2007, which acknowledged both her impact as a global fashion icon and her musical accomplishments. From her early days as a pop genius to her later position as a high-fashion icon, Kylie's style development has consistently enthralled designers and the fashion industry as a whole. When she received the 2017 Icon Award from the British Fashion Council, her lasting impact on fashion was further cemented. Her longstanding commitment to fashion and her ability to continuously alter her image in ways that are true to her individuality while still aligning with the industry's shifting trends were recognized with this award. Kylie's impact on fashion has grown to be as well-known as her music, thanks to everything from her trademark gold hot pants to the lavish couture ensembles in her music videos and live performances. Kylie has also gained a lot of notice for her charitable endeavors. She became a vocal supporter of cancer research and awareness after being diagnosed with breast cancer in 2005. She has now utilized her platform to advocate for early detection and collect money for cancer research after her personal struggle with the disease turned her into a symbol of hope for many. Kylie's services to the arts, notably her advocacy work in the health sector, earned her the French Ordre des Arts et des Lettres (Order of Arts and Letters) in 2008.

In addition to advocating for cancer, she has supported issues pertaining to HIV/AIDS awareness, children's welfare, and other humanitarian endeavors. In 2010, Kylie received the GQ Men of the Year Awards' "Charity Champion" accolade, further acknowledging her charitable endeavors. Kylie's dedication to charitable causes has persisted as a fundamental aspect of her public persona. She frequently uses her celebrity to promote concerts and fundraising events, such as her appearances as a headliner at the Sydney Gay and Lesbian Mardi Gras and "Children in Need." For her contributions to music, Kylie was named an Officer of the Order of the British Empire (OBE) in 2011. Her contributions to the arts and her impact on popular culture around the world were greatly recognized by Queen Elizabeth II, who bestowed this accolade upon her. For Kylie, receiving the OBE was especially significant because it was a formal acknowledgement of her influence on British entertainment and music, a nation that has been crucial to her career. Kylie received Australia's highest civilian distinction in 2019 when she was named an Officer of the Order of Australia (AO) in recognition of her outstanding contributions to the performing arts and her support of nonprofits. This honor was given in appreciation of her remarkable career in music and entertainment as well as her continuous community service initiatives.

# Marking Three Decades of Success in the Entertainment Industry

In a field that frequently values short-term success above long-term accomplishment, Kylie Minogue's capacity to endure is among her most impressive career traits. Being a presence in the entertainment business for more than 30 years as of the 2020s is a testament to Kylie's versatility as an artist and the steadfastness of her fan base. In addition to continuing to put out new songs throughout the past thirty years, Kylie has managed to stay relevant by redefining herself and her sound to suit the changing tastes of the pop scene. In 2017, Kylie received the "Legend Award" at the annual GQ Men of the Year Awards, marking a formal celebration of her 30-year career milestone in the music industry. She was honored with this award for her decades-long contributions to philanthropy, fashion, and music, as well as for being a timeless character in popular culture. In honor of her decades-long impact, especially within the LGBTQ+ community, she was given the "Music Icon Award" at the Attitude Awards that same year. Golden, an album that blended her characteristic pop sound with country music influences, was released in 2018 to mark Kylie's 30 years in the music industry. Golden, which peaked at number one on the UK Albums Chart, was a commercial triumph and demonstrated Kylie's ability to stay creative and relevant as she approached her fourth decade in the business.

The album's lead song, "Dancing," which combined reflective lyrics with lively music and further demonstrated Kylie's talent for reinvention, became another fan favorite. Kylie's consistent success on the charts has also contributed to her longevity in the entertainment world. Her ongoing appeal and significance are demonstrated by her remarkable achievement of becoming the only female artist to have a number-one album in the UK for five consecutive decades. Kylie has continuously demonstrated her ability to adjust to new musical trends while remaining loyal to her roots as a pop singer, from her debut album in the late 1980s to her 2020 release, Disco. Her live performances, where she has remained a dominant force on the global touring circuit, have matched her consistent economic success. Massive crowds have continued to attend Kylie's concerts; her Kiss Me Once Tour (2014) and Aphrodite: Les Folies Tour (2011) have become career highlights. One of the most prominent music festivals in the world, Glastonbury Festival, had Kylie as the main act in 2019. The successful performance, which took place 14 years after she had to postpone her initial Glastonbury participation due to her cancer diagnosis, represented her tenacity and the steadfast love of her fan base. Her continued popularity was further evidenced by the fact that her Glastonbury set became the most-watched performance in the festival's history. Kylie has continuously been one of the best-selling female musicians of all time in terms of album sales. She is one of the best-selling musicians in the world, with over 80 million recordings sold worldwide as of 2020. Sales are simply one indicator of her impact on pop music; another is the effect she has had on upcoming generations of musicians who look up to her as an inspiration. Kylie has won multiple lifetime achievement honors over her career, including the Brit Awards' "Outstanding Contribution to Music" prize in

2020. Her outstanding contributions to the music industry over the previous three decades were once again recognized with this prize.

# CHAPTER 16: KYLIE MINOGUE: A LIFE BEYOND THE STAGE

One side of Kylie Minogue's complex existence is her career as a musical sensation. In addition to her accomplishments in music, she has had success in acting, creating fragrances, and running other businesses. Each of these endeavors demonstrates her adaptability and solidifies her reputation as a cultural figure. From her early television days to her current status as a business entrepreneur, Kylie has proven her capacity for innovation and adaptation, impacting not only the music industry but also other creative domains.

## Acting Career

In 1979, Kylie Minogue won her first role on the Australian television series The Sullivans, marking the beginning of her acting career as a teenager. But what really made her famous was her portrayal of Charlene Robinson in the serial drama Neighbors. Neighbours, which debuted in 1986, helped launch the careers of numerous performers and became a cultural sensation in Australia and the UK. Viewers were captivated by Kylie's portrayal of the vivacious mechanic Charlene, especially when it came to her on-screen romance with Jason Donovan's character, Scott Robinson. One of the most unforgettable events in television history is still the famous 1987 wedding of Charlene and Scott. Kylie's acting career continued after she left Neighbours in 1988 to focus on her music career. Her ability to move from television to film was demonstrated in her 1989 film debut in The Delinquents, a love drama set in the 1950s. Kylie was nominated for the Australian Film Institute Award for Best Actor in a Leading Role because of the film's positive reception in Australia and its establishment of her as a legitimate actor. Kylie made an appearance in the 1994 movie Street Fighter, which was adapted from the well-known video game. Despite the film's mixed reviews, Kylie's portrayal of Cammy White was noteworthy and contributed to her expanding body of work. She played herself in the 2001 movie Bio-Dome, which starred Pauly Shore and Stephen Baldwin, showcasing her humorous side. Even though it wasn't a box office hit, it demonstrated Kylie's versatility as a filmmaker. In 2007, Kylie made her television comeback as a guest on the British series The Kylie Show, which included skits and musical performances. Her acting career also included a noteworthy performance as Astrid Peth in the 2007 Christmas special "Voyage of the Damned" on the Australian television series Doctor Who. The episode introduced Kylie's art to a new audience and was a critical and financial success. Kylie has indicated a desire to resume acting in more significant parts in recent years. She still has a deep enthusiasm for performing, and her experiences on stage and television continue to inform her creative pursuits.

## Fragrance Ventures

Additionally, Kylie Minogue has had a big impact on the fragrance sector. When Kylie Minogue Darling, her debut fragrance, was introduced in 2006, it was warmly received and soon became a best seller. The fragrance, which was characterized as a combination of fruity and flowery elements, suited Kylie's fan base and reflected her lively attitude. The success of Darling launched Kylie's wide-ranging fragrance range and solidified her position as a major force in the beauty industry. Kylie Minogue produced a number of new perfumes after Darling's success, such as Kylie Minogue Sweet Darling (2007), Kylie Minogue Pink Sparkle (2008), and Kylie Minogue Glamorous (2010). With distinctive components that appealed to her audience, each fragrance demonstrated her developing ingenuity and sense of style. In addition to their alluring aromas, Kylie's fragrances are renowned for their chic packaging, which reflects her sense of style. In order to further establish her brand in the fragrance industry, Kylie revealed her partnership with the French perfume firm in 2015. Inspired by her album of the same name, she started Kylie Minogue Kiss Me Once. Through this collaboration, Kylie was able to expand her audience and make a name for herself as a successful businessman in the cosmetics sector. The reasons behind Kylie's success in the fragrance industry include her strong brand identification, her awareness of her fan base, and her capacity to produce goods that complement her persona as a confident and glitzy pop star. Her reputation as a prosperous businesswoman has been cemented by the multiple honors and recognitions her fragrances have garnered.

## Business Ventures

Kylie Minogue has demonstrated her business savvy by pursuing a variety of ventures outside of performing and fragrances. She has worked with a number of businesses and brands, using her connections to forge fruitful alliances. One noteworthy collaboration was with Love, Kylie, an Australian fashion retailer that debuted in 2006. Fans could imitate her looks thanks to the collection's apparel, which was influenced by her distinct style. The brand's popularity demonstrated Kylie's influence on fashion as a pop culture figure. Its goal was to offer stylish yet affordable apparel options for ladies. In 2010, Kylie and Sainsbury's, a UK-based grocery store chain, collaborated to introduce a line of products called Kylie's Kitchen, which included cookware, cooking advice, and recipes. Fans were able to interact with her personally through this endeavor, which highlighted her love of food and wellness. Through the collaboration, she was able to expand her brand into other industries and establish a lifestyle brand that went beyond music. Through her companies, Kylie has also engaged in charitable endeavors, collaborating with nonprofits to promote a range of causes. Her dedication to giving back to the community is demonstrated by the substantial amounts earned for cancer research through her fragrance line partnership with the Cancer Council Australia. Kylie has always pushed the limits of production and originality in her live performances and tours, demonstrating her business mentality. Her concerts have revolutionized the live music experience with their intricate choreography, staging, and graphics, making them legendary. Her ability to produce captivating events that connect with fans was demonstrated by the Golden Tour in 2018 and the Kiss Me Once Tour, which was a great success in 2014.

## Her Influence on the Entertainment Industry and Other Creative Fields

Kylie Minogue has had a significant and varied influence on the entertainment sector. She was among the first female singers to combine pop music with theatrical aspects, and as such, she has encouraged many performers to accept their uniqueness and use their creativity to express themselves. In the music industry, Kylie's ability to reinvent herself over the course of her career has established a precedent, proving that longevity requires adaptation. Her impact is also seen in the fashion industry, where designers and trends have been influenced by her recognizable style. Kylie has always been on the cutting edge of fashion, from her earliest days wearing denim shorts and crop tops to her most recent haute couture looks. Her distinct sense of style has impacted designers including Christopher Kane, Dolce & Gabbana, and Jean Paul Gaultier. She has been welcomed by the fashion industry, which sees her as a trailblazer and muse. In the LGBTQ+ community, where she is regarded as a gay icon, Kylie's influence is particularly noticeable. She has gained admirers in the community thanks to her advocacy for LGBTQ+ rights and her frequent appearances at Pride celebrations. LGBTQ+ listeners find great resonance in Kylie's music, which frequently celebrates themes of love and inclusion. Other artists have also been inspired to embrace inclusivity and promote equality by her work with the LGBTQ+ community. Apart from her impact in music and fashion, Kylie's forays into scent and beauty have provided avenues for other artists to investigate financial prospects beyond their primary professions. She has made it possible for musicians to launch their businesses in the beauty sector and inspired a new wave of artists to use their platform to pursue business endeavors.

# What the Future Holds for Kylie as a Cultural Icon

The future is bright as Kylie Minogue continues to establish herself as a cultural phenomenon. Over the course of her more than thirty-year career, she has proven to be incredibly resilient and adaptable. She has been able to stay relevant in a field that is always changing thanks to her ability to adapt to shifting audiences and trends. Kylie continues to be dedicated to her music, charities, and business endeavors as she takes on new tasks and endeavors. Kylie has made hints about potential future musical and artistic endeavors. Fans may anticipate more avant-garde work from her in the years to come, as her love for creating and singing songs is still very strong. She has been enthusiastic about pursuing new artistic paths, such as working with up-and-coming musicians, in recent interviews. Her desire to work with others and try new things shows how committed she is to maintaining an interesting and unique sound. Additionally, Kylie is probably going to keep up her charitable endeavors, utilizing her position to advocate for worthy causes. As she tries to improve society, her involvement with LGBTQ+ advocacy and cancer research is anticipated to grow. Kylie's dedication to charity is consistent with her morals and strengthens her reputation as an inspiration to her followers. Future generations of artists and producers will surely continue to be influenced by Kylie Minogue, a cultural icon. Her legacy is one of resilience, inventiveness, and empowerment. Kylie's capacity to uplift and engage her audience will continue to be a defining characteristic of her long-term success as she negotiates the changing entertainment landscape.

# CONCLUSION

Kylie Minogue is one of the most recognizable personalities in modern pop culture thanks to her journey across the fields of music, fashion, and personal reinvention. Kylie has handled the challenges of celebrity with poise and genuineness, starting as a child actor on Australian television and progressing to become a worldwide pop success. In addition to captivating audiences, her ability to consistently modify her voice, appearance, and artistic direction has established a benchmark for durability and flexibility in a field that is constantly evolving. Kylie has accomplished incredible feats in her career, which demonstrate her commitment to her art. Her reputation as a pop legend has been cemented by her run of number-one singles, albums, and standout performances. Every musical era demonstrates her adaptability and willingness to try new things, from the dance-pop hits of the late 1980s to the reflective tones of her latter work. Her ability to develop while remaining loyal to her artistic beginnings is demonstrated by the successful release of albums such as

Aphrodite, Golden, and Disco. Beyond her musical pursuits, Kylie has a significant impact on charities, fashion, and scent. Her dress choices frequently make headlines and influence trends, demonstrating her status as a style icon. In addition to giving her a new avenue to interact with her fan base, her entry into the fragrance market has established her as a shrewd businesswoman. Her dedication to changing the world is evident in her charitable endeavors, especially her support of the LGBTQ+ community and advocacy for cancer research. As a cultural figure, Kylie is extremely significant, but her status as a homosexual icon is especially notable. The LGBTQ+ community finds great resonance in her songs and her demeanor, and her candor about her support of different issues has won her admirers worldwide.

As a reflection of her basic beliefs and the connection she has with her fans, Kylie's performances frequently function as joyous occasions when messages of acceptance and love flourish. Kylie Minogue is still a major player in the entertainment sector as she looks to the future. She is still motivated by her love of music and performing, and her spirit of entrepreneurship leads to new prospects. She will surely be guided in her future creative pursuits by the lessons she has learned throughout her career, including the value of authenticity, the strength of connection, and tenacity in the face of adversity. The tale of Kylie is one of self-determination, inventiveness, and unshakable commitment. Whether via her music, clothes, or charitable endeavors, her capacity to uplift others has left a legacy that endures throughout generations. Fans continue to honor Kylie Minogue's contributions to pop culture, serving as a constant reminder of the value of embracing change and following one's passions. Kylie Minogue's influence will endure in the constantly changing entertainment industry, and her artistic vision will be appreciated for many years to come. With a multi-decade career and a legacy that only gets richer with time, Kylie's life story is about more than just her music—it's about the lasting impact she has had on the world. As she continues to flourish and produce, her story acts as motivation for fans and aspiring artists alike, demonstrating that everything is achievable with skill, perseverance, and sincerity.

Printed in Dunstable, United Kingdom